Why dr____ ____ ____
than a crystal ball.
Find out . . .

* What it means if someone who has died appears in your dreams

* How Jeane Dixon forecasts history-making events through her dreams

* Why an open window may be a premonition of death—or escape

* How dreams can help you make the right career choice

* How dreams can help you create novels, movies, inventions, and more!

* Hundreds of dream symbols that reveal the hidden meanings in your dreams, including: backseat (being driven, not in control), black dog (instinctual desires, death), dolls (babies), house (the body or self . . . the grander the house, the grander the sense of self), shoes (female genitalia), telephones (communication with the deceased)

PLUS—the world's greatest dream prophesies from saints, world leaders, and famous psychics!

DELL BOOKS BY LAUREN LAWRENCE

Dream Keys

Dream Keys for Love

Dream Keys for the Future

DREAM KEYS FOR THE FUTURE

Unlocking the Secrets of Your Destiny

LAUREN LAWRENCE

A Dell Book

Published by
Dell Publishing
a division of
Random House, Inc.
1540 Broadway
New York, New York 10036

Dell books may be purchased for business or promotional use or for special sales. For information please write to: Special Markets Department, Random House, Inc., 1540 Broadway, New York, N.Y. 10036.

Dell® is a registered trademark of Random House, Inc., and the colophon is a trademark of Random House, Inc.

ISBN: 0-440-23479-4

Printed in the United States of America

Published simultaneously in Canada

August 2000

10 9 8 7 6 5 4 3 2 1

OPM

To Jack and Elaine

ACKNOWLEDGMENTS

Vast indebtedness to Pierre Salinger for taking time out of his busy schedule to write my foreword. Profuse thanks to all who offered up their fleeting dreams to be pinned down on a page in a book, especially Pierre Salinger, Arlene Dahl, Gale Hayman, Ivana Trump, Oleg Cassini, John Davis, Ludovic Autet, Heather Moore, Ghislaine Absy, and Katie. A note of gratitude to Beth Polish, President of Dreamlife.com, for welcoming me into Dreamlife's Web community as their dreams expert.

Special thanks to Carol Lupo for her inspired and expedient research and to my son, Graham, for his erudition and critical readings. Warmest thanks to Joey Reynolds at WOR and Herb Squire at WQXR for their kind support, and to my agent, Liz Berney, for her effort.

Appreciation to my editor, Danielle Perez.

Lauren Lawrence
New York City
January 18, 2000

CONTENTS

FOREWORD

)

November 19, 1963. I remember the day vividly. I was leaving for Honolulu and then on to Tokyo with six members of John F. Kennedy's cabinet to discuss the prevailing Vietnam problem and our new economic relations with Japan. I was always sent ahead of the President, six weeks earlier, to prepare his working schedule. Kennedy was supposed to go to Japan in late January 1964. He would have been the first President of the United States to do so since the end of the war.

On the day I was to leave, something morbid and terrible happened that left a vivid impression on my mind. I received a letter from a woman named Jeane Dixon, who told me, in no uncertain terms, that Kennedy should not go to Dallas, Texas, as he was planning. For she predicted President Kennedy was going to be killed in Dallas. I gave the letter to Kennedy. He shrugged and told me that his security was going to save him. On November 22, 1963, I was miles away. The rest is history. In grim retrospect, this was my first experience with prophesy, up close, and personal. Shockingly true.

In the next three decades I have had many dreams that turned out to be prophetic. Lauren Lawrence analyzes one that I dreamt back in 1982 when I was on vacation in Corsica. I had been covering terrorism for ABC and perhaps had taken my work to bed with me that evening. During my sleep a voice told me to be aware—the worst terrorist attack will occur in Paris, in August, in the last week. Realizing the importance of dreams with strong messages, I headed for Paris. The next morning a terrorist bomb exploded in a French-Jewish restaurant and killed twenty-one people. I was shocked that my dream had become a reality. Stranger still was my retelling of the dream to Lauren Lawrence on the afternoon of August 31, 1997. Several hours later the world would hear of the tragic death of Diana, Princess of Wales, in Paris, in August, in the last week. Lawrence questioned why I had picked the last day of August to tell her my dream, and she worried that my prophetic dream of '82 may have been speaking about a time in the future. Perhaps prophetic dreams have an afterlife. Perhaps Diana was terrorized.

Last year I had another prophetic dream. The British Open golf tournament was being shown on television. Excited about golf, I would go every morning into CNN Sports to watch the happenings each day. When the tournament ended Sunday night I had no idea who had won. That night I dreamt that someone called me from London: "Mark O'Meara has won the British Open." When I awakened the next morning I watched CNN Sports and discovered that Mark O'Meara had won. Once again my dream had mysteriously and unaccountably held the correct answer.

Lauren Lawrence's book is extremely valuable. It attempts to uncover the roots of prophesy and unearth what concealed cause it grows from. This book is a powerful learning tool. It reveals that dreams predict character traits, life direction, physical illnesses, and the outcome of relationships and events. Lawrence breaks down predictive dreams into understandable categories, cites numerous dream examples, and makes fascinating analyses.

If of late dreams have lost their Freudian significance due

to new distrustful scientists and their scientific views of the brain's functioning, Lauren Lawrence intelligently buffs the gleam back into dreams, and does not stop there. Her notable book's poignant psychological perspective puts a modern spin on the biblical dreams of Joseph, Jacob, Ezekiel, King Nebuchadnezzar, and Saint John. Every one of her exciting interpretations gives us pause. Many are chilling.

It is a fact that in their dreams, numerous people have made discoveries, written poetry, and come up with characters and the plots of novels. According to Lawrence, Robert Louis Stevenson's dreamworld not only recognized the condition of manic-depression but dreamt up its chemical cure as well. I marvel over the fact that this is entirely plausible and eagerly await my next sleep—to see what dreams may come.

Pierre Salinger
Washington, D.C.
May 22, 1999

PART I

Prophetic
Dreams

1

The Prophetic Dream

We know in part, and we prophesy in part.
I Corinthians 13:9

Confounding scientific reasoning, the majority of paranormal experiences or phenomena, such as prophesy, clairvoyance, astral projection, and ESP, remain either unverifiable, inconsistent, or unexplainable—and at best, in the realm of the hypothetical. Prophetic dreams, however, in that they come packaged in narrative form, may for the most part be interpreted and understood in conventional psychoanalytic terms, and can be apprehended with the provision of first having taken into account perceptual, intuitive, motivational, and emotional sensory factors.

Simply put, the prophetic dream is either a precognitive experience or an intuitive impression that delivers information, often via a clear mental image that is confirmed to be valid when it is eventually borne out. These prophetic dreams, however, appear to be outside the realm of human mental capabilities, as they are predictive communications supposedly received from beyond the impersonal environment. Such predictive abilities become accessible when the dreamer is made aware of inaccessible sensorial or visual events that lead to precognition (prior knowledge) of future events or appearances that are not immediately verifiable.

But after everything is dreamt and discussed, even the ordinary dream may be considered as a possible vehicle of prophesy—a universal key that connects us with our unconscious by accessing an otherwise unreachable plane, realm of perception, or experience. For it is from this unconscious realm that collective (in the Jungian sense), universal (as opposed to individual) remembrances emerge.

Universal remembrances are very different from individual remembrances. To be sure, whereas an individual remembrance is concerned with one's exclusive, personal, private past preserved in unconsciousness, the universal remembrance is concerned with the Jungian collective unconscious: one's shared, impersonal, public, world memory, in which lies the accretion of knowledge of all past events, and the concepts, images, thinking, and feeling processes of mankind. Both forms of remembrances are often subliminally perceived in a manner similar to a déja-vu experience that is intuited rather than observed. These remembrances reach us from the subliminal region of the subconscious in a symbolic format that may be examined in dream interpretation.

Similarly, it is in this unconscious realm of sleep that the deceased may revisit dreamers from the astral recesses of the universal remembrance. But in accessing this astral plane one has to transcend or attain a new level of consciousness, according to the mystic Eliphas Levi. Indeed, heightening consciousness may be none other than the transcendent function of dreams. For the dream is a way of actualizing this astral plane, this highly charged unconscious plateau wherein cosmic memory is housed and wherein the dreamer enters into unconscious communion with the world memory. In other words, the dream may be seen to stimulate suprasensible energies: *Indeed, dreaming may well be the closest thing we do in our everyday lives that may be considered mystical.*

TO BE OR TO KNOW WHAT WILL BE: THAT IS THE QUESTION

In as much as Enrico Fermi's particle theory has spoiled the notion that seeing is believing, it no longer seems mandatory to believe what one sees. For this reason, the issue of whether certain dreams are prophetic or simply intuitive cannot be determined simply by interpretation or by the occurrence of foretold events. Every prophetic dream may have at its core a serendipitous coincidence, a psychoanalytic reason, or an intuitive essence. For the dream presents to our unconscious minds all that we have already witnessed or heard or experienced. We are constantly picking up external cues from our socio-emotional environment, and it is questionable how we interpret or how we personalize or emotionally translate this experience. Whether a dream has correctly predicted the future cannot be determined merely upon an examination of the evidence alone, as any good inquiry must admit probability or chance to its list of antecedents.

While it is certain that our unconscious contains the past, it is entirely a matter of conjecture whether it contains the future as well. Let us examine for one moment what remembering the future entails, for this bears great significance on the meaning and understanding of prophesy. If life is predetermined rather than free-willed, then destiny must be accepted as belonging to the realm of the past. This would mean that anyone who believes in determinism must necessarily believe that there is no future, but only an inescapable past, in that everything has already happened over time. In other words, the future is out there because it already has been or was.

As a dream, or particularly the unconscious, is nonlinear, it has neither temporal knowledge of past or present nor knowledge of spatial boundaries, as there is no contrast or distinction of time. This would allow the opposite sides of the spectrum, past and future, to be chasing each other's tail—the future would appear in the past and the past would appear in the future. Similarly, just as the past appears in dreams as the present, so the present may appear as the future. What better space than the unconscious to locate or relocate what is so far ahead that it is already behind us in an atmosphere where everything has already happened. This is the same space wherein the proverbial magician's rabbit is pulled pink-eared out of a black satin hat—the rabbit is always there, we just do not see it. The question remains: If time has no significance to the unconscious mind, then why are prophetic dreams so hard to believe, understand, or accept? If we can conceptualize Einstein's view of the circularity of time, then we can conceptualize an oxymoron: the previous future. This would be an easy way for us to deter-

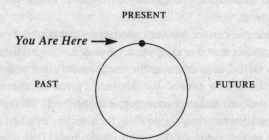

mine that the prophetic dream is anticipatory in nature. As seen in the time diagram on page 6, the future loops into the past.

Simply said, the prophetic dream is either a precognitive experience, a dream that wavers and buzzes around the dirt of the collective unconscious like a divining rod in search of a future that has already occurred, or a memory of an intuitive impression (as in déja vu).

FOUR TYPES OF PROPHETIC DREAMS

Prophetic dreams fall into two classes: the active and the passive. The active form contains subconscious perceptions (intuitive information) that are sensed but not apprehended during consciousness, and are expressed through movement and activity, symbols and images. The passive form, stripped bare of images and scenery, like the empty stage of a Beckett play or minimalist art, contains a vocal message or warning; the voice may be unfamiliar or recognized as coming from a deceased loved one. Both forms of dreams contain secret wisdom—but coming from where? Some say the prophetic dream conveys a realization of the will. I content myself with thinking that having a prophetic dream is like sleeping with the CIA, whose mysterious and secret agency has all the answers long before it releases them to the general public.

The first type of prophetic dream is presented as a *realistic dream*. Often the information conveyed is not in disguised form but in a clear, mental image (or voice), and has detailed content without unconscious elaboration (see Pierre Salinger's dream in Chapter 16).

The second type presents itself as an *unrealistic dream*. Often information is disguised, encoded, or veiled in symbolic form, in which a message is represented by a parallel situation, such as the biblical story of Pharaoh, who dreamt of "seven fat kine (cattle) and seven lean kine."

The third type of prophetic dream contains *both realistic and unrealistic* elements (see Jeane Dixon's dreams in Chapter 19). Most of these dreams, however, may be explained away as a chance event or what Freud would call *zusammentreffen* (coincidence), or attributed to an intuitive perception of the psyche. Yet, even though many prophetic dreams may be given psychoanalytic interpretations, there are those that simply defy being defined as anything other than paranormal occurrences. What is beyond hypothesis is that prophetic dreams (like ordinary dreams) occur when the dreamer is unconscious, undisturbed by the sensory stimuli of the environment, and when one's intellectual and emotional defenses are down.

The fourth type of prophetic dream is *the vision*: the wakeful dream in which the subject has a reverie that intersects consciousness midway between the preconscious and the unconscious, an experience similar to the drunkard's hallucinated sightings of pink elephants (see Chapter 9, Vision as Wakeful Dream).

From an intuitive standpoint, there is always the notion that the prophetic content of the dream experience has at its subconscious roots an antecedent (a daytime residue) from the day before that has triggered a predictive perception that, for whatever reason, is only realizable or obtainable in the sleeping unconscious. The intuitive dreamer processes or builds up the past information to the point where it becomes a stepping-stone with a view—a heightened position for looking over shoulders and forecasting an outcome.

As consumer-driven advertising has already realized the power of subliminal presentation in the selling of products, the prophetic dream is a prototypical consumer in that it has been influenced by subliminal material along the way. Unbeknown to an individual, our body language is giving off clues. One may think one is hiding an illness from public view while one is actually presenting or telegraphing subtle changes in one's behavior or attitude that may act as signifiers. Although these changes are not consciously perceived by any prospective dreamer, they may register unconsciously and subsequently emerge in a precognitive dream of the prospective dreamer's friend's illness or death. Similarly, one may try to hide a nasty side of one's personality or a ruthlessness, and while these characteristics may be overlooked by a prospective dreamer, they may surface in his unconscious dream. This is a case in point of the future reaching into the dreamer, as opposed to the dreamer reaching into the future, and of a perceptual process in which a subliminal, unidentified environmental or emotional stimulus is perceived by an individual and mediated during his unconscious sleep state. In this scenario, the dreamer is a passive receiver (like a patron of the Home Shopping Network!).

Similarly, a dream that prophesies the death of a loved one (someone emotionally or physically close to the dreamer) may indicate nothing more than the emotional bond existing between the two, a bond that has been found (particularly in studies with identical twins who are separated) to be conducive to prophetic, unspoken communication.

INSIGHT VS. PREDICTION

Insight or subliminal observation is strongly related to prediction if we take into consideration the fact that surface appearance is not always an indication of the intentions or motives that are lying beneath. The unbitten apple does not externally reveal its core, and yet on some level the core is intuited. Even though the wakeful mind makes many a character delineation in a nanosecond, for the most part, due to stimuli distraction or conscious restraint, we remain unaware of these complex observations, as they do not proceed into conscious thought but rather are submerged into the unconscious. Mulled over in leisure, however, these overlooked insights resurface in dreams in the form of formulated opinions that serve to predict the character of an individual before that character becomes known over time.

For example, here is a predictive dream that was dreamt by a businessman, Mr. L, who had interviewed a prospective applicant for an executive position within his firm. While waiting to be interviewed, the applicant, Mr. K, had warmed up several secretaries with his dry sense of humor. During the interview, the busy and impatient Mr. L was won over by Mr. K's frequent compliments and his warmth and sincerity, and after assessing his extensive resume was favorably inclined to hire him. That night Mr. L had the following dream:

Mr. K was sitting behind a large desk partially hidden by stacks of books and a clutter of paperwork. No longer jovial or congenial, he was speaking in a gruff manner on the telephone. His mouth curved downward, very hard and thin as a line. His jaw was clenched. He was bragging that the money he had stolen from his previous company would never be traced back to him as he had erased his tracks. As he spoke, he was erasing numbers on some sort of balance sheet and blowing the erasures into my face. A red glow painted the whole room, which was soon enveloped by thick smoke. Through the smoke I noticed the playing cards on his desk, particularly the black

jack of spades, which was very large and in dispropor-
tion to the rest of the deck. I was feeling anxious and
alarmed as I closed the door.

The next day, after Mr. L discussed his dream with his psychoanalyst, he decided that the dream was based on an irrational comparison he had made to a former employee with whom he had had a bad business association. The former employee's last name coincidentally began with the letter K, and he had also been an avid poker player.

After several years, however, it proved apparent that Mr. K had been stealing accounts from Mr. L's firm and laundering large sums of money. He had covered his tracks by erasing and substituting false figures in the books, and in the process managed to put Mr. L out of business.

Mr. L sadly recalled his former dream, which was clearly predictive. In this instance, the dream was an indication of the truth. Mr. L's unconscious dream impressions of Mr. K had proved entirely accurate, as they correlated with the sinister character and actions that Mr. K would later reveal. Because the clues were all within the dream, they were consciously available, but they were either repressed or dismissed in favor of an expedient hiring. In looking back, the red glow that appeared in the dream cut through the jovial exterior and highlighted a devilish, deceptively nasty, and thieving Mr. K, shrouded in a smoke screen. The black jack was indeed a knave. Clearly, although the cards were on the table, it was easier for Mr. L to simply close the door, as he did not want to see.

As we have seen, there is often a misperception of a situation or a situational bias that prevents the truth from being consciously known. Further complicating perception is the fact that perception is not always veridical but can be largely a construction based on an observing individual's expectation or founded on personal belief systems or emotional sensory states—in other words, an assessment is formulated based on past experience or probability. Often there are deficiencies of recall, in that stimuli often register without evoking conscious sensation, temporal determination, or critiquing; an individual may pick up informational cues along the way that are long forgotten and that, when reinstated in the unconscious dream, appear as prophetic.

Saint Thomas Aquinas, among numerous others, has theorized that the unconscious contains a somatic knowledge or awareness of the physical workings of the body that may factor into prophetic prediction. The following prophetic dream of a thirty-three-year-old man in seemingly good health typifies this view:

> *I dreamt that the filtering system in my pool must have been damaged or clogged, as the water remaining in the pool was stagnant and dirty, like sewer water. There were some rusty cracks in the sides. And there were leaves and debris floating on the surface. Flies were buzzing around as I was trying to clean up the pool.*

The following year the man was diagnosed with kidney and liver cancer that would prove to be fatal. Did his unconscious mind have the awareness of his inner disposition, which it then symbolized as a failure in plumbing? Or was the dreamer despairing over an inward sense of personal stagnation? Perhaps consciously there was surface recognition of a dissolute existence, as the dream reveals that debris is floating on the surface of his pool.

Yet from a purely paranormal perspective, the prophetic dreamer is tuning in to future information the way a radio picks up frequencies from far away. It is said that the bond is weakened between the physical body and the astral body (or etheric body), which is the seat of the personality of the prophetic dreamer. Supposedly it is this weakened bond that allows the dreamer to wander off spatially and temporally to various places and people. It is for this reason that the dream state of a prophetic dreamer is said to be a deeper state of awareness than wakeful consciousness; such dreamers delve beyond the surface information, without a time/space continuum, to a depth that has an immediate and powerful relationship with the world—a relationship that becomes guiding, as it is specifically hidden from our own conscious intellect. For example, here is a purely prophetic dream that was dreamt by a young Greek dressmaker before she was to be married in Greece:

> *A tall man in a black suit comes in front of me. He puts his arm around my waist and holds me. From where I am standing I see the whole New York City skyline. I recognize the Empire State Building, and in the distance the Statue of Liberty. The man says, "You are mine. You must marry me."*

Months after this dream, the young dressmaker arrived in America and found herself in New York City, standing in the precise location that the dream depicted. She then made the acquaintance of a tall stranger in a black suit, who was quite taken with her. According to the dreamer, the stranger's face was an exact double of the face of the man within her dream. They married shortly after this meeting.

Of course, it could be argued that the dream was merely a manifestation of a wish fulfilled by the willful determination of a young dreamer eager to move to New York City, and that the dream divulged the dreamer's dissatisfaction with her present fiancé and her need for liberation (she recognizes the Statue of Liberty). Yet the dream remains an uncanny event in that the face of the strange man pictured within the dream is the actual face of the man that the dreamer marries. Once again, however, the cause of such an occurrence may be chalked up to the determination of the dreamer to seek out the man of her dreams. In other words, this man must conform to what she construes as a desirable type of male.

Indeed, the prophetic dream may only be transcribing information that embodies truths our consciousness dismisses or merely does not recognize. In other words, the prophetic dream may be an instrument of specialized perception and/or attention—a horse without blinders that focuses on the peripheral rather than the direct view.

The question remains: Is the prophetic dream merely a manifestation of intuition based on what is perceived, or is the dream prescient, based on foreknowledge? In the manner that Freud regards ESP as an atavistic communicating phenomenon that may have been needed for survival in past epochs, so the prophetic dream may be viewed as an antiquated, vestigial mechanism of evolution. (Similarly, Jung refers to the figurative language of dreams as being a survival from an archaic, or as Nietzsche has put it, a phylogenetic old mode of thought.) Yet social biologist Edward Wilson speaks about a predictive gene in our biological makeup that has grown in our evolutionary scale of development in a way that transcends its past ability—such as was inherent in our cavemen predecessors, who intuitively moved away from threatening areas, refrained from ingesting poisonous foods, or awakened in times of impending danger. In conclusion, who can say to what depths and expansions of intelligence our continuing evolution will bring us? Maybe the lack of human precognition in the mind of present-day man will be considered by future generations as a relic of the last several decades of the twentieth century, with its heavy reliance on the non-supernal, fast-food machinery of easy information, the deus ex Macintosh, IBM, or Dell.

2

A Historical View
of Prophetic Dreams

ore often than not, we find the word "prophet" inextricably related to a simple mortal of unerring faith who has been chosen, it seems, for the express purpose of giving revelation, of revealing God's divine will. In this way, the word "prophesy" denotes a sense of the sublime and extraordinary, and singles out the prophet, soothsayer, or clairvoyant dreamer who possesses this dauntingly mysterious power of seeing ahead—this unexplainable power to perceive things that are naturally beyond the range of the human senses—as the subject of much controversy, which is often dangerous.

Aside from Judeo–Christian biblical views that accepted prophetic dreams as messengers of divine insight, possessing this kind of foreknowledge has, at times throughout human history, proved lethal and has resulted in the immolating of Saint Joan of Arc and numerous others on the burning stake, for having such power has often made the visionary seer suspect of guile, sorcery, and even witchcraft.

What could be more vexing? A prophetic dream must be like having the heightened auditory sense of the dog, which can hear high frequencies far above the range of the human ear, or like having the x-ray vision of Superman, who can penetrate leaden boxes and reveal their unseen contents. The difference is that the prophetic dream is more ordinary; it only has to see through paper—the paper weeks, months, and years of a calendar diary.

Are these dreams a result of a dreamer's acute intuitive insight, or are they manifestations of occult phenomena? Are the prophetic dreamers schizophrenic or merely vividly imaginative? Let us examine what literary, philosophic, religious, and scientific scholars have had to say on the subject.

From the moment after the first recognized dream some three thousand years ago and up until the present there has been immense and varied speculation as to the understanding of this phenomenon. From what realm, mundane or heavenly, does the dream emanate? And other than being the supplier of good breakfast conversation, what purpose does a dream serve? Is the dreamer morally responsible for his actions within the dream experience? And are these actions mere wish fulfillments that are in and of themselves causes of future actions?

The primitive West African Ashanti people's view of dream interpretation is based on personal responsibility, in that dreams are considered real experiences. The Ashantis have, in fact, been known to fine married dreamers who have blatantly committed adultery within the confines of their dream bedrooms—most probably because the sexual action within the dream may have been thought to be prophetic, as a wish that would need to be fulfilled.

The Mohave, Yuma, and Navaho Indians conceptualize

the unconscious dream world as an infinite, invisible doorway to the deceased and pay strict attention to whatever otherworldly exhortations of departed souls they may hear within the dream narrative, as they are believed to be premonitory.

In ancient times, the Greeks (see the section on Aristotle in Chapter 21), for the most part believed in the predictive function of dreams, particularly in relation to the diagnosing of physiological problems. Various symbols were recognized for representing somatic symptoms or ailments. The unconscious dreamer was thought to possess a deeper awareness of the functioning of his body—his physical plane. This awareness or sensing of bodily changes would translate into the dream narrative and thereby allow the dreamer, upon waking, to foretell a future illness or physical malaise. In this view, the dream itself is a symptom that prefigures the manifest onset of illness.

This theory is entirely similar to the nineteenth-century philosophic view presented by Schopenhauer, which influenced a number of pre-Freudian writers, such as Krauss, Scherner, Volkelt, and Strumpell, all of whom espoused a relationship between somatic stimuli and dream images in which dreams are reduced to organically determined sensations. (Even Freud has acknowledged that in many instances dream life has proved analogous to pre-existing but as yet unrecognized conditions of psychical illness in wakeful life, which can be taken to mean, in no uncertain terms, that unconsciousness knows something before consciousness does.) For example, according to Strumpell, a flying dream is an image based on an unconscious association of the mind with the stimulus produced by the rising and sinking of the lobes of the lungs. Similarly, according to the early Greeks, a flying dream that reveals a difficulty in flying, in which the flier becomes heavy and languid, means there is reason to suspect that a somatic illness is forthcoming.

Artemidorus, however, in his second-century A.D. book on the interpretation of dreams, although adhering to the nonpsychological belief that a dream is physiologically predictive, understood that prophetic dreams are ones that are also able to uncover in unconsciousness a truth—any truth—that has been overlooked during consciousness. In addition, he gives a name to a more spiritually based type of prophetic dream whose purpose it is to inform, calling it an oracle: a revelatory experience during sleep through which information is willfully imparted to the dreamer by an angel, a saint, or God himself. As an example, he mentions the visitation dream of Joseph of Nazareth, who heard an angelic presence clarify the forthcoming birth by the Holy Virgin Mary.

A fourth-century author, Synesius of Cyrene, has written that within each dreamer is the instrument of divination (see Chapter 25, The Inside-out Theory of Prophesy). In other words, man is his own diviner, his own oracle, and should listen to the voice of his dream as it communicates the miraculous counsel within all of us.

Talmudic scholars believe in the predictive ability of dreams, particularly in dreams that occur during the morning hours; morning sleep is deemed less deep than at night, as the sleeper is closer to wakeful consciousness and therefore reason and the possibility of rational judgment. At such times, the dreamer has a greater interpretative ability and thus a better chance to elicit either a personal insight or an insight into others in a way that is predictive of future actions or occurrences. There is also the assumption that, since the unconscious dreamer is removed from himself or emotionally detached, he will have an impartial objectivity to view and fathom an unbiased future. Yet this predictive quality is based on the intuitive faculty rather than the prophetic or uncanny.

In the thirteenth century, Maimonides stated that prophetic dreams, although formulated on one's reasoning powers, are the result of the action of the imaginative faculty during sleep. Yet it is imperative for the dreamer to understand how to separate the rational from the symbolic. In other words, the interpreting of the prophetic dream symbols is all-important (see Chapter 20, on Edgar Cayce) in that the structural symbols are like our DNA, with the declarative knowledge of what we are made of and, most importantly, of who we will become.

In what could be termed a modern view, Saint Thomas Aquinas writes that what may be deemed a prophetic dream may actually be the cause of future occurrences, in that the dreamer is sufficiently influenced by his dream to act in accordance with the self-knowledge he has gained within the dream. In theory, this idea is likened to the psychological dynamic behind the self-fulfilling prophesy, in which an anxiety may make an individual act in a certain way that will bring about the dreaded effect of that which has initially made him anxious. He debates whether the dream is the causative agent of the future or merely the perceiver of what will be. For example, in reality a boyfriend may have anxiety over his girlfriend's faithfulness. He then dreams that his girlfriend is unfaithful, which causes his unconscious feelings of distrust and jealousy to surface into consciousness to the extent that there is continual fighting between the two that eventually breaks up the relationship. When the girlfriend finds another lover, the prophesy within the dream is fulfilled!

Saint Thomas Aquinas observed that dreams are sometimes inside us and sometimes outside ourselves. Like Artemidorus before him, he believed that the inward (internal) cause of the dream involves the physiology of the body in that the somatic disposition is able to formulate a mental attitude (or picture) that is consistent with the dreamer's state of health and that is predictive (diagnostic) rather than prophetic. The outward or spiritual cause of the dream is affected by environmental conditions, such as heat or a cold draft, or an external messenger, as its cause may involve the presence of a heavenly body or visitation. The spiritual cause is thought to be sometimes referable to God, who has angels reveal certain things to humans in dreams, yet it is also sometimes conversely referable to demons, who reveal things to those who are of an evil disposition.

Hobbes, Kant, and Voltaire are in agreement with the nonpsychological pre-Freudians in assuming that dreams predict as a result of somatic stimuli—the worse the dream, the more disordered the stomach! Indeed, these physiological approaches to understanding dreams that prognosticate differ drastically from views prevalent at the start of the Christian era that propounded dreams as illusive religious phenomena—as vehicles (messengers) of divine insight expressed symbolically.

Somewhat skeptically, Coleridge felt that dream predictions are coincidental in nature and that they derive from associative powers. In other words, he believed that dreams are fully sensical, being based on the senses (particularly those of somatic origin), as they often reveal in advance a diseased physical system within the dreamer. Coleridge's somatic view of prophetic dreams, however, was no doubt a product of personal experience: the remembrance of his father's premonitory dream that foretold his death. The father's dream was as follows:

> *Death appeared to [me] as he is commonly painted,*
> *and touched [me] with his dart.*

The week after Coleridge's father's morbid dream (of which at the time Coleridge was not aware), the nine-year-old Coleridge was awakened by his mother's scream upon realizing that her husband was dead, whereupon Coleridge, in semi-consciousness, proclaimed to himself "Papa is dead," without ever knowing the meaning of his uncanny fore-knowledge. The only thing that Coleridge remembered was his father's complaining of a pain in his bowels.

It must be assumed that Coleridge's dream concept en-deavors to explain his father's prophetic dream and his own foreknowledge of his father's death, which is why there is a strong focus on the subtleties of observation, which are often lost during consciousness and often retrieved during sleep. Although Coleridge cannot prove whether an inner sense (which for the most part remains undeveloped) exists within the mind, he endows this sense with having the power of presentiment.

His theory is formulated on his belief that all external senses are remembered through corresponding objects in the mind. In other words, the eye can envision an object well be-fore the object of sight becomes identifiable or is understood with any distinction. He questions the existence of a corre-sponding power within the soul—a power to envision the fu-ture through the memory of a corresponding sense of the past. In this way, the power of prophesy may lie in provoking a spiritual (sensual) excitation to erupt from an otherwise dormant faculty.

He plays with outward perceptibility, which in fact can be nothing more than a false inner sense of what is only an outward imperceptibility. He offers an interesting perception: His library window, which looks out on the lawn, the bushes, and the trees, is directly opposite his fireplace, which, as evening darkens, is able to reflect the light of its flames upon the lawn, the bushes, and the trees and make them appear aflame.

In a manner of speaking, the aforementioned perception reveals that something is transposed on something else, or seen in another way. Yet the light of the flames is needed to accomplish this visual unreal perception. Thus, at very bottom, Coleridge's theory of prophetic dream perception depends upon the gathering of symbols and one's imagination, for one's imagination contributes to every act of perception.

Ralph Waldo Emerson, in theorizing that dreams are made out of the maturation of opinions not consciously carried out into statements, is in effect saying that we are already in possession of the facts but choose to leave them unassembled. All the pieces of a jigsaw puzzle are on our table of consciousness, but a disassembled picture cannot be seen. In other words, the prophetic dream gives back what is already in the mind from daily observances that remain repressed or unexpressed.

Emerson believes that the dream is unbiased and therefore truthful, which is why the prophetic dream is able to recognize personal character or the behavioral traits of others, which often appear in ways that do not manifest themselves consciously. Because the dream recognizes these forces underlying our actions and behavior, it can predict future actions. This is to say that the prophesy is always contained or latent within the reason of the individual. Yet, in a spiritual vein, Emerson confides that a dream may offer hints that are thrown out from an unknown intelligence.

Most interestingly, Henri Bergson believes that when memory or thought processes are unfixed or unguided and are uninvolved with any action or environmental sense, a meditative union is produced between the memory and the sensation that may give rise to a prophetic notion.

3

The Predictive Dream

Bringing dream interpretation up to date is the most recent view of Hobson's activation-synthesis biological model, which thumbs its nose at the psychological approach to dreams and worships the scientific. In short, Hobson would have us believe that dreams are the stuff of all things cellular and molecular. The dream is considered a symptom of a meticulous brain's good housekeeping; it is likened to an after-hours office maid who cleans up after all the workers have gone home for the night, reorganizing, filing, and editing stored information. When the external environmental stimuli are at their lowest, the brain is inwardly activated. The cleaning woman has flicked up the switch on the silent, darkened office of the night, and the lights are awash with dreams.

Insistent on Hobson's biological model, social biologist **Edward Wilson** rebukes the interpretative value of dreams and particularly Freud's approach, describing dreams as random and meaningless "hallucinations" without context. In *Consilience*, Wilson gives a detailed explanation of the physiological characteristics of the dream state, a description that is inclusive of the triggering mechanism of the acetylcholine nerve cells that begin to fire in the brain stem, like anxiety-provoking gunshots. It is somewhat surprising, however, to find that the finical Wilson makes mention of but refrains from even questioning the value of the movement of the eyeballs during the REM state of sleep—the shallow period of sleep when dreams are formed, when there is no other movement, as motor paralysis has set in, and the body is paralyzed. It seems entirely reasonable to suggest that there must be some inherent reason for the eyes to be able to remain free to move during dream time, especially since the eyes are shut. For the eyes to be given the perk of motion when the immobile body is virtually shut down, there must be something vital to be seen in our dreams.

Along this line of reasoning, some researchers have tentatively put forth the suggestion that REM sleep may have a profound Darwinian function. These researchers have noted that dreams improve responses basic to survival. Indeed, Wilson offers up a concession that the brain may be genetically predisposed to invoke recurrent dream images. This brings to mind Freud's instinctual drive theory and the Jungian archetypes.

Interestingly, over the centuries there seems to be a continued genetic predisposition to dream fearfully of serpents. In fact, serpent imagery may be considered an instinctual relic of the past, which would mean that dreams of warning are in the service of human survival. The dreaming caveman who is awakened by his primordial fear of the serpent, at a time when the serpent is far away enough for him to run from it, is having a predictive dream. Generally speaking, one might even say that the whole notion of survival is formulated on wired-in predictive knowledge.

According to Wilson, a predictive gene insures that humanoids will always have ten fingers and ten toes. A predictive gene also guarantees that, in order for interpersonal communications (seeing and speaking) to happen in the present, a specific sequential pattern of events must occur, from chemical surges to electrical impulses over time, from seconds to minutes. Technically, being able to see ahead of ourselves—to predict in advance—would necessitate that we slow down the action enough to witness events that have already happened. But in order to accomplish this feat, Wilson says we will have to learn to function in "biochemical time" in addition to "organismic time." To comprehend the universe, we will need to view the space we are in from its respective time frame, for only at this point will our vision or view become immense enough to encompass a whole city. (The event of slowing down time is depicted in a novel scene from the movie *Contact*, in which Jodie Foster, while enclosed in her space vehicle, experiences approximately eighteen hours away from earth in what is actually and unaccountably clocked as a fraction of an earth second.) This as yet unachievable stratagem may typify the kind of advanced brain system at work—albeit unbeknown—within the mind of a prophet or divulge the mechanism behind the prophetic dream in a manner that would satisfy scientific inquiry.

A prophesy is expected to come true in that it is the receiving body of what is perceived to be determining outside information. A prediction is a step down from prophesy: Based on cognitive informational assessment, the expectation of its occurrence is speculative rather than determined. A predictive dream is actually an unconscious insight that is expressed to the dreamer in the symbolic and imagistic form of its narrative, an insight that consciousness will learn afterward. Thus, a dream that predicts is similar to a prophetic dream in that it sees or is cognizant of something ahead of consciousness.

While remaining anchored to the psychological vein that pumps blood through the heart of the psychoanalytic community, **Eric Fromm's** dream ideology diverges somewhat from the Freudian instinctual drive theory in order to reflect upon the rational, predictive value of dreams.

It is often said that dreams possess a predictive function particularly in relation to the diagnosing of physical and even mental illness (see Edith Rockefeller's dream in Chapter 17). Fromm acknowledges that during sleep a dreamer is closer to his physical being than during consciousness, as there is immersion in the self in a paralyzed state of immobility. Without the distracting intrusions of the external world to draw upon, it is likely that the dreamer's focus is turned inward. At this time, a physical change, no matter how subtle, will upset the fine tuning of the body and be noticed at once; it will merge within the dream in symbols that, when translated, will predict somatic occurrences. Pending more extensive study, Fromm limits himself from saying to what degree dreams manifest illness through their superior insight into the body during sleep.

Yet Eric Fromm believes in the existence of a rational, cognitively based predictive dream, as opposed to a prophetic one. Based on the inference that all current events have a way of extending themselves into the future, predictive dreams are linear. Predictive dreams, therefore, are rationally accepted, as they neither belong to the realm of the uncanny nor depend on telepathy or religious divination. Predictive dreams draw upon and present a logical chain of both conscious and unconscious inferences.

As examples of the rational, predictive inferences that can

be drawn from prophetic dreams, Fromm analyzes the biblical dreams of Joseph. Joseph's first dream elicits hatred from his brethren in that the dream prophesies his dominion over them. Joseph's dream is as follows:

> *We were binding sheaves in the field, and, lo, my sheaf arose, and also stood upright; and behold, your sheaves stood round about, and made obeisance to my sheaf.*

Joseph's second dream makes an even bolder pronouncement and is told to his father along with his envious brethren:

> *Behold, the sun and the moon and the eleven stars made obeisance to me.*

Whereas the first dream depicts Joseph's ascendancy over his brothers, the second dream nails down, as it were, his utter and complete domination. Both dreams can either be interpreted as angelic, God-given revelations, or analyzed as the dreams of realization of a young man who is coming to terms with his talents, for the dream is the vehicle that allows Joseph to assess or predict that he will outshine his siblings. This is Fromm's whole point of view. Within a psychological framework, the ultimate planetary obeisance is interpreted as a projection of Joseph's unconscious desires or wish fulfillments in that cosmic domination is thematically typical of childhood dreams, in which feelings of grandiosity crop up as frequently as sheaves in the field in a defense against helplessness and feelings of dependency.

Similarly, it may be said that dreams are the medium that allows Joseph to predict his later accomplishments, in that the voice that appears in Joseph's dreams is none other than his own. Fromm does not focus on the nature of Joseph's competitiveness but rather emphasizes his reasonable, moral desire to lead (see Part II, Biblical Dreams: A Psychoanalytic Perspective). Thus, Fromm's unconscious is not necessarily irrational, as it may often express itself in predictive, rational ways.

In Fromm's interpretation of biblical dreams, Pharaoh's warning dream of the devouring, ill-favored kine is predictive rather than a message sent by divine powers, as Joseph would have it. It is predictive to the extent that Fromm believes Pharaoh had to have had conscious, intuitive knowledge of the land and the fertility of the soil. In other words, Pharaoh's unconscious mind is able to mull over information culled from consciousness and formulate what amounts to a predictive outcome. In agreement, Artemidorus views Pharaoh's dream as an expression of his conscious insight.

Primitive people have long thought that dreams provide prophetic insight into the future, and there even exists in the modern world a real human need to believe in the mystical unknown. Taking this into account, it is still highly unusual to stumble upon a credited social scientist or two who believe in prophetic or predictive dreams. Nevertheless, **F. R. Freemon,** author of *Sleep Research: A Critical View*, actually classifies prophetic dreams into three workable categories. In the first one, "after-the-fact dreams" are culled from a large storehouse of previous dreams that suit the outcome in that they "jell with the facts"; in the second one, "statistical dreams" are remembered if the prediction actually occurs and forgotten if it does not come to pass; in the third category, "inner knowledge dreams" assist dreamers in personal recognition, wherein something useful is learned about themselves that is being aggressively repressed or overlooked during wakefulness. The third category is of particular interest in that it recognizes the predictive value of dreams; it espouses their function of giving dreamers a glimpse into a possible future. These predictive dreams are formulated on personal scrutiny of the dreamer's lifestyle, his behavior, and his actions, so that conclusions are drawn as to where these actions and behaviors will lead the dreamer.

Social scientist **W. C. Dement**, in *The Functions of Sleep*, reveals a predictive dream of his own that saved his life. The dream was dreamt during what must have been a hazy period in Dement's life when he was smoking three packs of cigarettes a day. His dream was as follows:

> *I coughed up blood. I had an x ray; my lungs were full of cancer. I felt poignantly the intense reality of the premature termination of my life, and then I woke up.*

In that Dement was given the opportunity to objectively experience his gruesome physical decline, a decline in which he actively played a part, he was made sufficiently aware within the dream of a life choice that should have been patently and consciously obvious. Dement stopped smoking as a result of his dream, which he believes to have been a predictive warning.

In conclusion, a predictive dream is one that has an internal authority—a willful authority granted by a presence of mind during conscious yet unrealized perceptions. The predictive dream represents man's inherent desire to discover his future before his future discovers him.

PART II

**Biblical Dreams:
A Psychoanalytic
Perspective**

4

Dreams of
Joseph

In the Bible, Joseph is depicted as a man of exceptional and extraordinary talent. Most importantly, the Bible reports him as having had prophetic dreams—all of which came to pass—and the interpretative skills of a prophet. In biblical times, dreams were not considered as psychological entities but rather as God-given messages. This is why Joseph says to Pharaoh, "God has shown Pharaoh what he is about to do," before Joseph interprets Pharaoh's dream.

Yet there is a strong predictive element in the biblical dreams that may account for the outcome. As we have previously noted, predictive dreams are rationally accepted, as they neither belong to the realm of the uncanny nor depend on telepathy or religious divination. Predictive dreams draw upon and present a logical chain of both conscious and unconscious inferences.

Many rational predictive inferences can be made from prophetic dreams, along with psychoanalytic assessments. Take, for example, Joseph's dream of greatness, which elicits hatred from his brethren because the dream prophesies his ascendancy over them. Is this not the youngest and weakest sibling's *cri de coeur* to become a powerful entity or an adolescent attention grabber? The dream certainly reveals and fulfills Joseph's wish to stand out from the crowd and be noticed. In psychoanalytic terms, the dream presents a well-crafted overcompensation for feelings of helplessness and dependency. Joseph's dream is as follows:

> *We were binding sheaves in the field, and, lo, my sheaf arose, and also stood upright; and behold, your sheaves stood round about, and made obeisance to my sheaf.*

From the perspective of physical development (height, specifically) there is certainly the wish to rise—to grow taller than one's siblings so as not to be literally or metaphorically looked down upon. This is why Joseph dreams that his sheaf arose—the sheaf is the symbol for Joseph himself. Yet, as a sheaf weighs little, its upright posture is often dependent upon the shifting moods of the wind and upon the sturdiness of its shaft. If the sheaf is firm, it stands upright or erect; otherwise, its top will often droop over. Thus, the sheaf of Joseph is a substitution for the male phallus, the symbol of strength and potency. The sheaves of his brethren that stood round about Joseph's sheaf depict him as being the center of attention. The sheaves that bend in obeisance are being stripped of their vitality; this is the inner striving of Joseph's adolescent character to aggress. The dream is predictive to the extent that it reveals Joseph's manifest personality and his ideas of grandeur and competitiveness, for his character traits are what govern his actions and behavior; they insure the desired outcome within the dream—the wish for recognition and the homage of obeisance. What is most importantly revealed is Joseph's ambition to lead, for this is what allows him to attain his future position of authority.

Joseph's second dream, told to his father and his envious brethren, reinforces his need to be recognized and heeded:

Behold, the sun and the moon and the eleven stars made obeisance to me.

As previously mentioned, of upmost importance is Joseph's ascendancy over his brothers, and in a larger sense his need for dominion over his realm.

Viewed in this way, Joseph's dreams are a visionary or prophetic medium that allows him to accurately predict his later accomplishments. In that the voice that appears in Joseph's dreams is none other than his own, Joseph is goading himself on. The eleven stars are the brethren—the sun and the moon symbolize his mother and father. The dreams clearly state Joseph's aspiration and unconscious intention to command praise and outshine his family.

Joseph's reputation as a prophet develops through his uncanny ability to interpret dreams. Joseph interprets the prisoner's dream (cited below) in the following manner. While imprisoned, Pharaoh's chief butler dreamt:

Behold, in my dream a vine was before me, and in the vine were three branches; it was as though it budded, its blossoms shot forth, and its clusters brought forth ripe grapes. Then Pharaoh's cup was in my hand; and I took the grapes and pressed them into Pharaoh's cup, and placed the cup in Pharaoh's hand.

Joseph interprets the dream in the following manner: "This is the interpretation of it: The three branches are three days. Now within three days Pharaoh will lift up your head and restore you to your place, and you will put Pharaoh's cup in his hand according to the former manner when you were his butler."

The dream clearly reveals the solicitous nature of the butler and signifies that even unconsciously his desire is to serve and nurture his master. The wine is a symbol for blood and suggests that the butler is willing to give—to squeeze out or "press"—his blood for his Pharaoh. Thus, as the dream testifies to the butler's good nature, it is indeed predictable to expect that he will be taken back into Pharaoh's good graces. Similarly, the butler's dream positively attests to his reemployment—he envisions himself back at work, with Pharaoh's cup in his hand.

The following is Pharaoh's chief baker's dream:

I also was in my dream, and there I had three white baskets on my head. In the uppermost basket there were all kinds of baked goods for Pharaoh, and the birds ate them out of the basket on my head.

Joseph's interpretation is as follows: "This is the interpretation of it: The three baskets are three days. Within three days Pharaoh will lift off your head from you and hang you on a tree; and the birds will eat your flesh from you." Both interpretations miraculously come to pass as prophesies predicted by Joseph, as it is Joseph who correctly understands and interprets the two dreams. But were these interpretations intuited, or were they based on divine knowledge?

While the butler's dream is objective, in that the dream is not self-consciously involved or concerned with the butler but rather only immersed in the life of the Pharaoh and his daily needs, the baker's dream is subjective in that it is self-centered. The baker is depicted as negligent and uncaring, as Pharaoh's food is leisurely pecked at and eaten by birds without so much as a contemptuous swipe or waving of the arms on the part of the baker. As the food is Pharaoh's, it may symbolize Pharaoh himself and the baker's unconscious wish to see harm come to his master from above. As the dream is seen to reveal character traits, it is reasonable, therefore, to predict that the baker will not be forgiven by Pharaoh.

Upon the butler's hearing several years later that Pharaoh is in need of having a dream explained, he remembers the imprisoned Joseph's interpretative skill and recommends him to his master. Released from prison, Joseph interprets the following two dreams of **Pharaoh**:

Pharaoh dreamed; and, behold, he stood by the river. And, behold, there came up out of the river seven well-favored kine and fat-fleshed; and they fed in a meadow. And, behold, seven other kine came up after them out of the river, ill-favored and lean-fleshed; and stood by the other kine upon the brink of the river. And the ill-favored and lean-fleshed kine did eat up the seven well-favored and fat kine. So Pharaoh awoke. And he slept and dreamed the second time: and, behold, seven ears of corn came up upon one stalk, rank and good. And, behold, seven thin ears and blasted with the east wind sprung up after them. And the seven thin ears devoured the seven rank and full ears. And Pharaoh awoke, and, behold, it was a dream.

Joseph interprets the dream in the following predictive way:

The seven good kine are seven years: the dream is one. And the seven thin and ill-favored kine that came up after them are seven years; and the seven empty ears blasted with the east wind shall be seven years of famine. This is the thing which I have spoken unto Pharaoh: What God is about to do he sheweth unto Pharaoh. Behold, there come seven years of great plenty throughout all the land of Egypt: and there shall arise after them seven years of famine; and all the plenty throughout shall be forgotten in the land of Egypt; and the famine shall consume the land; and the plenty shall not be known in the land by reason of that famine following; for it shall be very grievous. And for that the dream was doubled unto Pharaoh twice; it is because the thing is established by God, and God will shortly bring it to pass. Now therefore let Pharaoh look out a man discreet and wise, and set him over the land of Egypt. Let Pharaoh do this, and let him appoint officers over the land, and take up the fifth part of the land of Egypt in the seven plenteous years. And let them gather all the food of those good years that come, and lay up corn under the hand of Pharaoh, and let them keep food in the cities. And that food shall be for store to the land against the seven years of famine, which shall be in the land of Egypt; that the land perish not through the famine.

As earlier mentioned, Fromm believes that Pharaoh's warning dream of the devouring, ill-favored kine is predictive rather than a message sent by divine powers, as Joseph would have it. It is predictive only to the extent that Pharaoh had conscious intuitive knowledge of the land and the fertility of the soil. In this reasoning, Pharaoh's unconscious mind processes information culled from consciousness and formulates what amounts to a predictive outcome. Artemidorus also views Pharaoh's dream as an expression of Pharaoh's conscious insight.

The most salient perception is that insight is related to prediction. Therefore, Joseph's dream interpretations reveal his tremendous empathy and innate wisdom. It may be said that Joseph interprets Pharaoh's visionary dream as an expression of the Pharaoh's anxious mind. The Pharaoh may have remembered serious droughts that had occurred in the past and that these periods of time contrasted greatly with more prosperous times of rich agricultural fertility. Indeed, Pharaoh may have unconsciously brought these two memories together and realized that agricultural cycles are based on seasonal shifts in climate. Similarly, if Pharaoh were a control freak—the type of person who needs to be prepared for any eventuality and necessarily be atop any given situation—he would have had to have been aware of climate fluctuations and would have remembered and dreaded former droughts, of which there were many.

5

Nebuchadnezzar's Dreams

[God] gives wisdom to the wise ...
and knowledge to those who have understood.

DANIEL 2:21

The Bible records that King Nebuchadnezzar had a dream so perplexing and troubling that he told it to no one—not even the court magicians, astrologers, or sorcerers of his day—but rather insisted that they make known his dream to him, along with its interpretation. Only if the dream be told would the King believe its interpretation to be true. Because of the impossibility of this demand, those summoned before Nebuchadnezzar replied, "There is not a man on earth who can tell the King's matter; therefore no king, lord, or ruler has ever asked such things." They continued, saying, "It is a difficult thing that the King requires, and there is no other who can tell it to the King except the gods, whose dwelling is not with flesh." Sufficiently angered, the King gave the decree to kill all the wise men of Babylon. When Daniel was told by the captain of the King's guard the nature of the decree, Daniel asked the King to give him time to tell the King the interpretation of a dream he had not even heard.

The Bible records that the secret dream was revealed to Daniel in a night vision so that the wise men would not be killed in Babylon. But before Daniel explained the King's dream, he mentioned, "There is a God in heaven who reveals secrets, and He has made known to King Nebuchadnezzar what will be in the latter days." Then Daniel did the impossible—he recounted and interpreted the King's dream, saying that the visions of his head upon his bed were these:

You, O King, were watching; and behold, a great image! This great image, whose splendor was excellent, stood before you; and its form was awesome. This image's head was of fine gold, its chest and arms of silver, its belly and thighs of bronze, its legs of iron, its feet partly of iron and partly of clay. You watched while a stone was cut out without hands, which struck the image on its feet of iron and clay, and broke them in pieces. Then the iron, the clay, the bronze, the silver, and the gold were crushed together, and became like chaff from the summer threshing floors; the wind carried them away so that no trace of them was found. And the stone that struck the image became a great mountain, and filled the whole earth. This is the dream. Now we will tell the interpretation of it before the King.

Daniel astounded King Nebuchadnezzar by giving him a prophetic account of coming empires after his reign and told the King that he, Nebuchadnezzar, was given this prophesy by God. Nebuchadnezzar's dream, therefore, must be considered above any psychoanalytic interpretation, as the dream was never told but rather divinely given to Daniel. At most, we may make the claim that Daniel telepathically received the King's thoughts and was able therefore to know the dream and make an interpretation.

We can, however, interpret from a psychoanalytic

perspective the following prophetic dream of Nebuchad-nezzar, as the narrative is personal and introspective:

> I was looking, and behold, a tree in the midst of the earth, and its height was great. The tree grew and became strong. Its height reached to the heavens, and it could be seen to the ends of all the earth. Its leaves were lovely, its fruit abundant, and in it was food for all. The beasts of the field found shade under it, the birds of the heavens dwelt in its branches, and all flesh was fed from it. I saw in the visions of my head while on my bed, and there was a watcher, a holy one, coming down from heaven. He cried aloud and said thus: "Chop down the tree and cut off its branches. Strip off its leaves and scatter its fruit. Let the beasts get out from under it, and the birds from its branches. Nevertheless leave the stump and roots in the earth, bound with a band of iron and bronze, in the tender grass of the field. Let it be wet with the dew of heaven, and let him graze with the beasts on the grass of the earth. Let his heart be changed from that of a man. Let him be given the heart of an animal, and let seven times pass over him. This decision is by the decree of the watchers, and the sentence by the word of the holy ones, in order that the living may know that the Most High rules in the kingdom of men, gives it to whomever He will, and sets over it the lowest of men."

Nebuchadnezzar's symbolic dream is one of transforma-tion and spiritual development, as the dream reveals the very depths of his nature, his aims and intentions. The huge tree is the dramatic elaboration of a thought or masturbatory fan-tasy: It is a formidable phallic symbol—an erect projectile of the earth that signifies male energy, strength, power, and domination. Yet the tree is depicted as a powerful guardian that stands watch over the grass of the earth—over its dominion—and as such is a symbolic representation of the King himself. The King is the phallic representative, having "reached the heavens." The King is the commanding authority figure, an attention grabber or eye stopper, in that he can be seen "to the ends of all the earth." But with his head in the clouds, the King or tree has gotten too big for its britches, and the clarity of the King's mind has been compromised.

Significantly, the personified tree represents the overreaching nature of the King and his egomaniacal need to ascend above his worldly kingdom. Yet, even with fruit abundant and heavenly birds on his branches, there is conflict or trouble in paradise. Hence, the emergence of the guardian superego, the psyche's regulatory system, in the guise of the watcher, whose worrisome conscience finds fault with the King's grandiose and immodest thoughts.

The voice of this "holy one"—the self-conscious, internal voice of the King—orders the tree to be chopped or cut down to size, as the dream is an attempt to compensate for the King's megalomania, which develops into psychosis. The branches must be cut off, as the King's ego must be trimmed. If he is to survive, he must be separated from his reign and all that gives him material sustenance; he must stand alone with his stump and roots in the earth—his deeply rooted anxiety. The leaves are stripped off in an effort to gain sight of the source from which the tree comes—the Holy God.

The dream makes the realization that the King is merely a stump bound by a band of iron and bronze; this is the bondage of the King to his crown. Toward the end of the dream, the tree that is formerly referred to as the pronoun "it" is personified as "him" and revealed as a man—a man who must humble himself by grazing with the beasts of the earth, and feeling with the heart of an animal. For the dream reveals how those who are "Most High" can fall as easily as fruit from a tree.

The dream is predictably somatic and prophetic in that it comes to pass: Nebuchadnezzar had a mental breakdown and periodic bouts with madness, whereupon he believed himself to be an animal and went out in the fields to graze. The Bible reports that he gave up his rule and wandered through the countryside "wet with the dew of heaven," in communion with nature, in search of humility and truth.

6

Jacob's
Dream

Freud views biblical dreams as merely "artificial" constructions of "imaginative writers" and thus makes no attempt at interpreting their symbols. Yet anything symbolic—whether it be a dream or an action—is fully interpretable and reveals something about the dreamer or person involved in the action (see my chapter on Actualized Dreams in *Dream Keys: Gaining Insight into Your Love Life*). Dreams from biblical times are symbolic and reflective of a way of thinking; they reveal the needs of the dreamer. What is extraordinary is that the dreams mentioned within this text (with the exception of Daniel's) were in reality so insightful that they have proved historically accurate and thus prophetic. In regard to Daniel, at present biblical scholars cannot verify Daniel's existence. Jacob's lineage, however, has proved verifiable.

The Bible records that Jacob dreamt the following prophetic dream in a place that he called Bethel (which literally means House of God):

*And behold, a ladder was set up on the earth, and its
top reached to heaven; and there the angels of God
were ascending and descending on it. And, behold, the
Lord stood above it and said: "I am the Lord God of
Abraham your father and the God of Isaac; the land on
which you lie I will give to you and your descendants.
Also your descendants shall be as the dust of the earth;
you shall spread abroad to the west and the east, to the
north and the south; and in you and in your seed all the
families of the earth shall be blessed. Behold, I am with
you and will keep you wherever you go, and will bring
you back to this land; for I will not leave you until I
have done what I have spoken to you." And when
Jacob awoke from his sleep he said, "Surely the Lord is
in this place, and I did not know it."*

As the beginning of a dream usually reveals the object (in
symbolic or disguised form) from which the stimulus arises,
we find ourselves struck with Jacob's need to personify
heaven or the continuation of a world that one cannot see beyond the clouds. The symbol of a common ladder is viewed
as a bridge or connecting vehicle to the heavens and to the
house of God. For without a physical means or material arti-
fact such as the ladder there can be no ascension. Rather than
through meditation or prayer, a ladder is set up on the earth as
a means to gain access to the ultimate heights and link oneself with God. The ladder is the construction of a connection
to a higher power.

As an image of ascension from the depths of humanity,
the ladder belies the agenda of the dreamer to succeed so-
cially, to come up in the physical world. Yet the lone dreamer
depends on the familial connections of his father, Abraham,
to the all-powerful, infinite parental authority of the Lord

God. For, as one individual, Jacob is weak and powerless, which is why he wishes to spread his seed and populate.

Thus, the dream contains a fulfilled wish: a gift of land and a promise that may be a self-fulfilling prophesy. The Lord gives Jacob and his descendants the land on which he lies and tells Jacob that his descendants "shall be as dust of the earth" and "shall spread abroad" in all directions—"all the families of the earth"—in God's blessing.

At the end of the dream when the visual symbols are nil, the bare narrative presents the actual dream stimulus itself— fear. When Jacob's descendants are symbolized as dust, an important function is served: A fear of death is eliminated, in that within death or dust a seed of life is found that brings the comfort of continuance. With Jacob alone and sleeping in a strange place, his dream may be seen as protective in nature, as it delivers confidence and assurance. Jacob need not fear, for he is told within the dream that he is not alone—God is with him wherever he goes.

7

Daniel's
Dream

The Bible records that "in the first year of Belshazzar King of Babylon, Daniel had a dream and visions of his head while on his bed." Chapter 7:1–8 of what the Bible refers to as Daniel's Vision of the Four Beasts is as follows:

> I saw in my vision by night, and, behold, the four winds of heaven were stirring up the Great Sea. And four great beasts came up from the sea, each different from the other. The first was like a lion, and had eagle's wings. I watched till its wings were plucked off; and it was lifted up from the earth and made to stand on two feet like a man, and a man's heart was given to it. And suddenly another beast, a second, like a bear. It was raised up on one side, and had three ribs in its mouth between its teeth. And they said thus to it: "Arise, devour much flesh!" After this I looked, and there was another, like a leopard, which had on its back four wings of a bird. The beast also had four heads, and dominion was given to it. All this I saw in the night visions, and

*behold, a fourth beast, dreadful and terrible, exceed-
ingly strong. It had huge iron teeth; it was devouring,
breaking in pieces, and trampling the residue with its
feet. It was different from all the beasts that were before it, and it had ten horns. I was considering the
horns, and there was another horn, a little one, coming
up among them, before whom three of the first horns
were plucked out by the roots. And there, in this horn,
were eyes like the eyes of a man and a mouth speaking
pompous words.*

Daniel's prophetic dream continues as a testimony to his
faith in God and in the power of righteousness, in what the
Bible records as the Vision of the Ancient of Days:

*I watched till the thrones were put in place,
And the Ancient of Days was seated;
His garment was white as snow,
And the hair of His head was like pure wool.
His throne was a fiery flame,
Its wheels a burning fire;
A fiery stream issued
And came forth from before Him.
A thousand thousands ministered to Him;
Ten thousand times ten thousand stood before Him.
The court was seated.
And the books were opened.*

Daniel's dream continues throughout 7:11–14:

*I watched then because of the sound of the pompous
words which the horn was speaking; I watched till the
beast was slain, and its body destroyed and given to the*

burning flame. As for the rest of the beasts, they had their dominion taken away, yet their lives were prolonged for a season and a time. I was watching in the night visions and, behold, One like the Son of Man, coming with the clouds of heaven! He came to the Ancient of Days, and they brought Him near before Him. Then to Him was given dominion and glory and a kingdom, that all peoples, nations, and languages should serve Him. His dominion is an everlasting dominion, which shall not pass away, and His Kingdom the one which shall not be destroyed.

In verses 1–8, Daniel is presented as a watcher, for his watching is what prevents him from active participation. At the outset, the dream reveals the ambitions of the dreamer (of man), which are quickly humbled as there is conflict between the self-interest of vanity and the humility of self-criticism. The beasts that come up from the sea (the unconscious) represent the emerging presence of the animal nature within man. The dream holds the remembrance of man's evolution from bestiality, and his human transformation; instead of crawling on all fours, he has an upright spine so he may stand on two feet like a man. The beasts are self-involved with gaining dominion through the devouring of "much flesh." In a mockery of humanity, the most dreadful and terrible beast has the eyes of a man and a mouth that is speaking pompous words.

In the Vision of the Ancient of Days, God is depicted as holding court, as the all-powerful father who will punish the disrespectful children, the indifferent beast that devoured, broke in pieces, and trampled with its feet (the very bottom of its nature) all in its path and the rest of the beasts for their transgressions. The books that are opened reveal the wish to receive prophesy, wisdom, understanding, and a moral code of ethics. The books prophetically prefigure the Bible.

In verses 11–14, the dreamer maintains his impassive stature as an onlooker (displacing his anger on another) by watching one enemy slain and given to the burning flame, and other enemies stripped of their dominions, taken away like so many toys as a measure of God's justice and retribution.

A particularly prophetic element of the dream alludes to the coming of the Christ, as he is referred to as the Son of Man. In a testimony of Daniel's faith, the dream states that His (the Son of Man's) is an everlasting dominion—one that can never be destroyed, for faith brings salvation.

As a whole, the underlying theme of the dream provides an explanation of the future, of cause and effect, of good and bad. There is no depiction of actuality but rather an imaginary expression. Taken as a revelation, Daniel's dream historically reveals what is to be. Yet his dream does not have to be a miraculous divination or a form of precognition for his unconscious to be able to predict a future situation based on a nonperceived conscious present set of circumstances. Taken as a warning, the dream reveals that religious persecutions will be remedied and that evil will be destroyed in the world. Ancient man dealt with his stressors by relying on his heightened instincts; a sense of control and order was replaced by one's faith in God.

Whereas a biblical interpretation reveals that Daniel's historically prophetic visions describe four empires that will rule the world until the might of God's Kingdom triumphs, a psychoanalytical interpretation views Daniel's dream as one of retribution and punishment, wherein God is called upon to reveal the secrets of the future and to still the anxiety of the dreamer. The antecedent of the dream is the ill feeling directed against Daniel and his people. The excess of punishment serves as a justification. Daniel may be the one who wants to do the destruction—to inflict punishment on his enemies and aggressors—but he does not want to suffer the consequences or admit to feelings of aggression. In that having something taken away is a symbol of dissociation, Daniel's dream promises that the bad will have their dominions taken away.

As each individual is oriented toward understanding his self and his human existence, Daniel personifies God with his offspring, the Son of Man. This is the symbolic figure of the Jungian Cosmic Man, a powerful image that embodies the human spirit and the mystery of its expression in our psychic reality. As mentioned previously, in a prescient sense the Son of Man is the foreshadowing of the coming of Christ.

The dream is involved with creation, destruction, and restoration. In that the dangers of the external world pose the threat of final destruction or elimination—in short, the ego's disappearance from the world—the ego seeks something immortal to get lost in, such as the Ancient of Days and the Son of Man.

8

Ezekiel's Visionary Dream

D uring the time when Ezekiel was among the captives by the River Chebar, he dreamt or envisioned that God informed him that he, Ezekiel, was the Son of Man, a term that was previously referred to in Daniel's prophetic dream. Ezekiel's mission is to confront the "impudent" and "rebellious" inhabitants of the house of Israel and deliver the Lord's warning. His dream in full, which would fill up many pages, is one of self-empowerment in that it imbues Ezekiel with strength and courage—the Lord God makes Ezekiel's face "strong against their faces" and his forehead "strong against their foreheads, like adamant stone, harder than flint." In another section of the dream (2:12) he is given the power of flight or is most certainly enlightened, as "the spirit lifted him."

The dream interpretation given below neither concerns itself with Ezekiel's own interpretation as is recorded in the Bible nor with the historical implications of the dream, but rather contents itself with an analysis of the beginning part only—for therein lies an extraordinary prophesy that miraculously foretells aviation, a prophesy that cannot be explained as anything other than divine knowledge. The following analysis is restricted to 1: 4–28 of Ezekiel's visionary dream. An abridged account follows:

> *Then I looked, and, behold, a whirlwind was coming out of the north, a great cloud with raging fire engulfing itself; and brightness was all around it and radiating out of its midst like the color of amber, out of the midst of the fire. Also from within it came the likeness of four living creatures. And this was their appearance: They had the likeness of a man. Each one had four faces, and each one had four wings. Their legs were straight, and the soles of their feet were like the soles of calves' feet. They sparkled like the color of burnished bronze. Their wings touched one another. The creatures did not turn when they went, but each one went straight forward. As for the likeness of their faces, each had the face of a man, each of the four had the face of a lion on the right side, each of the four had the face of an ox on the left side. . . . each of the four had the face of an eagle. . . . Their wings were stretched upward. . . . And each one went straight forward . . . wherever the spirit wanted to go, and they did not turn when they went. . . . Their appearance was like . . . the appearance of torches. Fire was going back and forth among the living creatures; . . . and out of the fire went lightning. . . . The creatures ran back and forth . . . like a flash of lightning. Now as I looked at the living creatures, behold, a wheel was on the earth beside each living creature with its four faces. The appearance of the wheels . . . was like the color of beryl, . . . their works was . . . a wheel in the middle of a wheel. . . .*

They did not turn aside when they went. As for their rims, they were so high they were awesome; and their rims were full of eyes. . . . When the living creatures went, the wheels went beside them; and when the living creatures were lifted up from the earth, the wheels were lifted up. When those went, these went; when those stood, these stood. . . . The firmament above the heads of the living creatures was like the color of an awesome crystal, stretched out over their heads. And under the firmament their wings spread out straight. . . . Each one had two which covered one side, and each one had two which covered the other side of the body. When they went, I heard the noise of their wings, like the noise of many waters, like the voice of the Almighty, a tumult like the noise of an army; and when they stood still they let down their wings. A voice came from above the firmament that was over their heads. . . . And above the firmament over their heads was the likeness of a throne, in appearance like a sapphire stone. . . . On the . . . throne was a likeness . . . of a man high above it. . . . From His waist and upward I saw . . . the color of amber with . . . fire all around within it; from . . . His waist . . . downward I saw . . . fire with brightness all around, like a rainbow in a cloud on a rainy day. . . . This was the appearance of the likeness of the glory of the Lord.

One might well imagine the wish of a captive to be able to sprout wings and fly away from imprisonment. Yet it is as if Ezekiel has seen a vision of the distant future at a time when men with wings rule the skies with their aircraft. The cloud that is personified with raging fire refers to the angry heavens, yet also depicts what we know of today as the bursting flames of the weaponry of war, of bombs and heavy artillery. The planes are perceived as creatures in that they are unexplainably huge and powerful entities or beings. They are perceived as living in that they are moving. The "living creatures" with "four wings" resemble the primitive airplanes that had "straight legs" to land on—the small wheels of the landing gear appear to Ezekiel as the soles of calves' feet. The metallic body of the plane, which is a composite alloy, is seen to sparkle like precious metal or bronze.

As the planes do not turn but rather fly straight forward, the nose of the plane is what is prominent and seen to resemble the face of a man. Animal imagery is used to explain what Ezekiel sees and hears. The animal descriptions of the face seem to be triggered by the following symbolic associations: The roar of the engines brings to mind the lion, the sturdiness and bulk of the form the ox, and the wings and pointed beak of the plane the eagle. Yet the various animals may also reveal man's character: The lion on the side of the right or righteousness represents courage and nobility, and the ox on the left side represents man's ignoble lower nature—stupidity and stubbornness. The eagle symbolizes man as a bird of prey.

The planes fly forward wherever their spirit takes them in a symbol of free will and human volition. Even though they torch the sky with their fire they do not turn or look back to see what they have done, which signifies the very worst in man—his impulsivity, lack of conscience, carelessness, and inability to learn from his mistakes.

The appearance of the wheels within the wheels symbolizes the tires of the plane or may refer to the movement of propellers, which assume a wheel-like shape. The rims that are full of eyes refer to the numerous windows along the body of the plane. The eye symbolism also signifies that the creatures are directed and need to see where they are going. This may also allude to the radar that flies a plane and the concept of a monitoring body.

As mentioned previously, the living creatures that lift up from the earth with their wheels beside them are unmistakably airplanes; the landing gear is positioned beside the plane during flight. In that the planes all take off together, they are flying in tandem, symbolic of military maneuvers or air campaigns. The wings that "spread out straight" are in flying position, with wings on either side.

The noise of their wings, which is perceived as "a tumult like the noise of an army," is the roaring sound of the engines, or perhaps a sinister battle cry of a future war. This is the voice that comes from above the firmament, which is interpreted by Ezekiel as coming from the Lord.

Verbal instructions of the Lord follow the visual portion of Ezekiel's symbolic dream or vision. Even within the dream there is secrecy, as Ezekiel is given a scroll that he is told to eat or digest, as a metaphor for understanding. The scroll is prophetic, as it symbolizes the Bible. Ezekiel is made a watchman for the house of Israel. He must warn the people of their impudent ways. The spirit enters him and "sets him on his feet," or sets him straight, as it were.

Ezekiel's dream foretells of a siege against Jerusalem and the house of Israel, which is not dissimilar to the 1967 Seven-Day War waged against Israel by the Palestinians, in a "whirlwind" that was "coming out of the North."

PART III

Visions

9

Vision as Wakeful Dream

Was it a vision, or a waking dream?
Fled is that music:—Do I wake or sleep?

JOHN KEATS

Theoretically speaking, the vision phenomenon is nothing more than a wakeful dream. The wakeful dream is an external/conscious dream that is outwardly produced and visualized, as opposed to a regular internal/unconscious dream that makes its usually nocturnal appearance within the body. It is witnessed with eyes wide open rather than viewed behind the confines of closed lids. Within the wakeful dream all the senses are engaged, unlike in an unconscious dream, in which the senses are inactivated and undisturbed by sensory stimuli. Indeed, it may be theorized that the dreamer is in a nether state in which consciousness intersects with that which is preconscious or subconscious.

Yet it may be that the dreamer has fallen into a meditative state of awareness that produces an ultra-consciousness (an extremely heightened consciousness) during the time that the wakeful dream or vision occurs. The value of the wakeful dream is that it is interactive; often there is questioning and answering, as one experiences other sensory stimulation during this experience.

SAINT JOAN OF ARC:
VOICES, VISIONS, AND LIGHT

There have been many historical sightings of prophetic visions, but arguably none have raised more controversy than the circumstances surrounding the visions of **Saint Joan of Arc** (Jeanne D'Arc), who was burned as a heretic for her beliefs. Joan claimed her visions were divinely inspired, for on many occasions she heard the voices of Saint Michael, Saint Catherine, Saint Margaret, and other heavenly beings, who advised her to come to the aid of the uncrowned King Charles VII of France in his battle against the English to affect a unification of his divided country.

While it can be argued that Joan's visions were the result of religious hysteria or even psychotic hallucinations, her vividly descriptive account of these visions, given at her trial in Rouen, remained steadfast in the face of scrutinizing examination. By examining these visions as wakeful dreams, we are presented with an entirely new way of examining the psyche of this mysterious and fascinating young woman.

Joan's First Vision

In *St. Joan of Arc*, John Beevers writes that Joan described her first vision as occurring when she was thirteen years old in the summer of 1424. It was the Archangel Michael whom she identified as her divine visitor. Vita Sackville-West writes in her *Saint Joan of Arc* that Joan recognized Saint Michael because he spoke with "the tongue of angels." Joan's account follows:

I was in my thirteenth year when a voice from God came to help me and guide me. At first I was frightened.

This voice came about noon in summer when I was in my father's garden. I had not fasted the day before. I heard the voice coming from my right from the direction of the church. I rarely hear it without seeing a light—and the light—always very bright—comes from the same side as the voice.

As a wakeful dream, the voice that comes from Joan's right is interpreted as being Joan's inner voice—the voice of the just. In terms of symbolic personal motivation, it is her voice that gives her direction. The light is the metaphoric sense of divine inspiration and also the lightness of being. What is interesting is that Joan was known to fast, and, in a physiological aside, it must be noted that fasting can bring about or produce feelings of light-headedness, which often precede black-outs or faints. Joan may have fasted on the day of the vision, as she clearly mentions that she had not fasted the day *before* the vision.

The Wakeful Dream as a Harbinger of Destiny

Until the moment when Joan of Arc first heard the voices, she had been living the life of a simple peasant girl in the French town of Domrémy. Joan was considered happy, robust, and sweet-natured—and an extremely devout Catholic. As the youngest of peasant farmer Jacques D'Arc's five children, Joan could neither read nor write but learned the Paternoster, the Credo, and the Ave Maria from her pious mother, Isabelle. She was also well versed in the lives of the saints. Given the child's strong religious upbringing and devout worship, it is reasonable to suggest that young Joan wanted to connect with heavenly beings via holy visions in order to assume an active part in God's plan. For devotion to God gave Joan a center of being, a direction in life so important to a young girl approaching her teens.

During the time of Joan's first vision, her native town of Domrémy was situated in the territory belonging to the Duke of Burgundy, who was allied with the English. However, in the midst of a prolonged conflict between France and England, Domrémy remained loyal to the French King, leaving the little village vulnerable to attacks by Burgundian troops. Although Joan was a simple peasant girl, albeit one heavily schooled in the teachings of the Church, she was not ignorant of the political climate in France.

In *The Maid of Orleans*, Sven Stolpe writes that the peasants of Domrémy spent a great deal of time discussing their trenchant political situation, and that Joan's father took a leadership position in adopting measures to protect the town. Therefore, concludes Stolpe, "Joan's childhood must have been filled with tales of violence and murder, attacks and plunderings, and her youth spent in a condition of tension and anxiety."

According to Sackville-West, the voice Joan first heard in her father's garden clearly explained to Joan her glorious mission:

> *Jeanne, you are destined to lead a different kind of life and to accomplish miraculous things, for you are she who has been chosen by the King of Heaven to restore the Kingdom of France, and to aid and protect King Charles, who has been driven from his domains. You shall put on masculine clothes; you shall bear arms and become the head of the army; all things shall be guided by your counsel.*

While it seems undeniable from Joan's personal accounts that divine forces were at work in counseling her, it is both historically and characteristically interesting to explore these visitations as wakeful dreams, as they bring another perspective to the portrait of Joan's life. The fact that young Joan, barely thirteen years of age, was living under extremely stressful conditions during a time of great political strife may account for the series of wakeful wish-fulfillment dreams/ visions in which Joan is seen to strive for self-empowerment in order to help her father in his mission as protector. The donning of masculine clothes is symbolic of her need to identify with her father and particularly with his leadership.

In that one's country is viewed as an extension of one's family, any normal adolescent feeling of powerlessness and dependency would increase in proportion to the societal conditions of political unrest at the time. Therefore, a wish-fulfillment vision or fantasy of the magnitude of the one experienced by Joan would serve as a transforming mechanism to endow Joan with feelings of power and self-reliance. Each successive vision or wakeful dream would serve as a self-fulfilling prophecy to inflame Joan with the will to achieve something extraordinary, as it would make her feel formidable enough to accomplish it.

Stolpe writes that by the time Joan was sixteen, the voices had become increasingly urgent, exhorting her to leave her village and fight for France. When she replied, "I am a poor girl: I do not know how to ride or fight," the voices insisted: "Receive your banner from the King of Heaven. Take it bravely and God will help you." Joan was convinced by these celestial voices that, with the Lord's help, she was destined to lead France out of its desperate situation with the English. Never mind that the tactical strategy for the campaign was probably established by the King's military advisors long before Joan ever took up the sword. When Joan finally directed an army of twelve thousand men at the age of seventeen, she believed that God was beside her in battle, rendering her both valiant and victorious in her efforts to drive the English troops from Orléans. Such is the power of faith.

Stolpe notes that Joan was well aware of a prophesy attributed to Merlin, the fifth-century Scottish visionary and magician of Arthurian romance. Merlin's prophesy, erroneously appropriated by the French, said, "A virgin shall descend on the back of the bowmen and with her shadow protect the lilies." The French interpreted the bowmen to be the English and the lilies to represent France, whose symbol is the fleur de lys—the lily flower. As Joan was cognizant of this prophesy, her visions as wakeful dreams may be manifestations of her fervent desire to be singled out as the one "chosen by the King of Heaven" to save her country.

At her trial, Joan testified that with each "visitation" she could clearly recognize, touch, and smell those who spoke to her. She told her prosecutors, "I saw them with these very eyes, as well as I see you." In *Saint Joan of Arc*, Sackville-West writes that Joan would embrace her spirits, presumably around the knees, as she herself was in most likelihood on her knees before them. Joan described her angels as having a fragrant smell—perhaps of lilies—and wearing beautiful crowns. They spoke to her in French, addressing her as Jeanne la Pucelle, *fille de Dieu*—Joan the Maid, daughter of God.

If Joan's visitations were wakeful dreams, externally produced and witnessed, her senses would be fully aroused and activated, unlike during sleep, when they are paralyzed. This would account for her being able to smell and embrace her spirits in addition to seeing them. We could then understand the blaze of light accompanying Joan's voices to be an aura that preceded her wakeful dream state, in which she was not entirely present in her surroundings.

There is no doubt that Joan was a keenly perceptive girl, possibly even clairvoyant. On her first visit to Charles VII she saluted him, although he had disguised himself to test her; on another visit, she convinced the King that she was sent by God by giving him a secret sign regarding his legitimacy. Indeed, Sackville-West notes that Joan even predicted her own suffering in battle, prophesying the very circumstance under which she would be wounded. Assessed as divine messages, each of Joan's prophesies was sent to her by God. Interpreted as a series of wakeful dreams, these states of semi-consciousness are what triggered her own precognitive abilities by bringing her own predictions to the conscious surface of her mind. Similarly, Joan's zealous devotion to God, coupled with her unshakable belief that she could save her people and her King, may be viewed as having stimulated strong unconscious strivings during consciousness, powerful urges that may have translated into mystical experiences: the visitations of celestial spirits as wakeful dreams.

EMPEROR CONSTANTINE: A VISION'S WAKEFUL DREAM LEADS TO A PROPHETIC DREAM

Although a wakeful dream can in itself be a vision, taking place while one is for all intents and purposes conscious, it can also lead to a prophetic dream that occurs during sleep. The prophetic dream serves to answer a question raised by the wakeful dream and sets the dreamer on a willful course of action.

An example of this phenomenon is well-documented in the wakeful dream of the Emperor Constantine, also referred to as *Constantine the Great*. Before any attempt at psycho-analytic interpretation, it must be clarified that the divinity of Constantine's vision of the cross of light is not in question. It is believed that this communication was from God himself; yet, in considering the vision as a wakeful dream, we arrive at a fresh viewpoint about a famous historical event of religious dimensions, an event that demonstrates the power of faith.

In *God, Dreams and Revelations: A Christian Interpretation of Dreams*, Morton T. Kelsey writes that Constantine prepared to liberate Rome by praying to God for help, and that he received a vision/wakeful dream of the cross of Christ that was to inspire his conversion in the aftermath of what would be a momentous and decisive winning battle:

> *And while he was thus praying with fervent entreaty, a most marvelous sign appeared to him from heaven. . . . He said that about noon, when day was already beginning to decline, he saw with his own eyes the trophy of a cross of light in the heavens, above the sun, and bearing the inscription* CONQUER BY THIS. *At this sight he was almost struck with amazement, and his whole army also, which followed him on this expedition, and witnessed the miracle.*

In *Dreamwork for the Soul*, Rosemary Ellen Guiley writes that although at this point in time Constantine had been proclaimed emperor by his troops, he still had to contend with his rival Maxentius. In that Constantine prayed fervently to God for succor, he must have viewed himself as being in a difficult and threatening situation.

His wakeful dream, as it was conscious and external, engaged Constantine's senses by allowing him to visualize the cross of light shining high in the sky, while remaining aware of both his surroundings and the time of day. He refers to this "most marvelous" imagistic cross of light as a trophy—his reward for calling on God in his hour of need. The inscription "Conquer by This" implies that victory is his for the taking. The optimistic and timely vision makes known the fact that, guided by the hand of God, Constantine will vanquish his opponent. Thus, Constantine's vision may be viewed as a self-fulfilling prophesy in that it empowers him and renders him a potent opponent to his challenger. Because of Constantine's willingness to fight in the name of God, God is his eternal and internal rescuer.

If this were an instance involving only a wakeful vision, Constantine may not have adhered to the omen or sign in the sky, as he was at first skeptical about the import of this apparition; thus he went to sleep pondering the validity of his vision: Had the Christ of God answered his prayers with a sign? As if in reply, God responded to his question with a prophetic dream. The dream is as follows:

And while he continued to ponder and reason on its meaning, night suddenly came on; then in his sleep the Christ of God appeared to him with the same sign which he had seen in the heavens, and commanded him to make a likeness of that sign and to use it as a safeguard in any engagements with his enemies. At dawn he arose, and communicated the marvel to his friends: and then, calling together the workers in gold and precious stones, he sat in the midst of them, and described to them the figure of the sign he had seen, bidding them represent it in gold and precious stones.

The sign that was revealed to Constantine in his dream was of the Greek letters χι/*hi (CH)* and *ro (R)* combined—

the first two letters of Christ's name—which thereafter became the symbol of the Roman Empire. The tangibility of the symbol, which was marked on his soldiers' shields by a rendering in precious stones and gold, was what gave Constantine a concrete representation of God's message. Carrying this actualized symbol into battle, he was further empowered and defeated Maxentius under what has been described as extraordinary circumstances. With the battle won, the prophesy was actualized.

Thus, as a result of Constantine's wakeful vision and dream, he became a staunch supporter of Christianity, and the first Roman emperor to become a Christian.

10

Nostradamus

Human understanding, being intellectually created, cannot see hidden things unless aided by a voice coming from limbo.

NOSTRADAMUS

In Lyons, in 1555, Nostradamus published his ten-volume book *The Centuries*—his almanacs of prophesy, which describe in symbolic quatrains all of man's future until the end of time. Amazing as it seems, more than four centuries later Nostradamus is still considered the prophet of our time, as many of his predictions are happening today—such as the fall of Communism, terrorist attacks, natural disasters, and the epidemic of AIDS. Nostradamus credited his awesome gift of prophesy to divine inspiration from a powerful, unnamed divine source. Nostradamus viewed language as a limiting and alienating element that restricted his powers of foresight, and he tried to free his conscious mind from distracting influences, the subversive stimuli of existence. Thus, although his foresight came through wakeful visions and not dreams, his philosophy on prophesy applies to both: Predictions arise in a mind unfettered by diversions.

Early on, Nostradamus was instructed in matters spiritual.

Through reading Socrates, Nostradamus was inspired onto the seeker's path of enlightenment through mind expansion. Through his mental seeking, Nostradamus was able to create his own self-imposed trances, like the clairvoyant Edgar Cayce (see Chapter 20).

He agreed with the medical discoveries of Paracelsus, who believed that both cures and diseases come from the unconscious mind. As Paracelsus had demonstrated that all man's conscious knowledge was useless, it is conjectured that Nostradamus used magical techniques to bypass consciousness and to conjure visions and ecstatic trance states, which came to him as wakeful dreams on specific astrologically favorable nights. Visions would come to him through the natural elements of fire or water—through fire gazing or water gazing, which, through concentration, must have brought him to a meditative state.

A RITUAL PRACTICE

In his voluminous writings, Nostradamus refers to a ritual practice prior to his trance state. In order to keep focused, he would sit in an upright position on a brass tripod whose legs were angled at the exact degree of the Egyptian pyramids in order to create a bio-electric force that he believed sharpened his psychic powers. He relied on the sense perception of smell: A brass bowl steaming with stimulating aromatic water rested on another brass tripod at his feet.

Between deep inhalations of steam, he began an undulating incantation. Through each long exhalation he emptied his spirit, mind, and heart of all wasteful anxiety and attained a harmonious state of tranquillity—a prerequisite for opening up the mental doorway to prophesy.

John Hogue, in *Nostradamus and the Millennium*, recounts Nostradamus' description of the first stages of his trance:

The prophetic heat approaches . . . like rays of the sun casting influences on bodies both elementary and non-elementary.

Dipping a laurel branch into the brass bowl, he anointed his foot and the hem of his robe. Then, seized by a sudden rush of paranormal energy, Nostradamus would find himself in another dimension, in which a voice came from limbo to direct him on his quest to get beyond intellectual understanding or consciousness. From the water or fire gazing, as if from a burning mirror, came a clouded vision of important future events. Nostradamus believed that the vision was achieved by a union with "the divine one," which was either God, the Jungian collective unconscious, Cayce's Akashic Records, or perhaps his own divine self. Most importantly, the ritual practice helped him overcome fear—the fear of surrendering to an immense power greater than himself, the fear of loss of control, of being overwhelmed by an ecstatic trance.

Nostradamus theorized that hidden things manifest themselves to the prophet by the following two means:

By infusion, *a clarification of light that overtakes one and makes possible divine revelation in one who predicts by the stars.*

By participation *or interaction with the divine eternity, by which the prophet can judge what is given to him through his own spirit through "God the Creator and his natural intuition."*

Of special significance is the dream-like symbolic manner in which Nostradamus wrote down his visions into quatrains, often relying on imagery and metaphor, on anagrams, reversals of words, literary devices such as the synecdoche, and ellipses. Like the displacement that often occurs within a dream, Nostradamus scrambled chronological order by listing nonsequential events. Names were hidden within normal words or phrases such that his prophetic quatrains need to be decoded or interpreted just as in dreams. Below are some of his more famous prophetic quatrains, along with analyses.

THE QUATRAINS

In 1559, King Henry II of France died during a jousting accident. Several years earlier Nostradamus had written the following quatrain:

The young lion will overcome the older one
on the field of combat in single battle.
He will pierce his eyes through a cage of gold
Two wounds made one. Then he dies a cruel death.

Nostradamus' quatrain may have personal significance in that he was raised for the most part by his grandfathers, spending a good deal of time separated from his mother, for whom he must have yearned. Thus, the young lion is the son overcoming his father, the older one, in a variation of the classic oedipal battle of blinding dimension—the father's eyes are pierced. The two wounds made one—the oedipal event and the subsequent blinding—summon a remembrance of the Sophoclean protagonist Oedipus Rex.

The next quatrain refers to the 1587 execution of Mary Stuart (Queen of Scots), who fled across the river from Scotland to England:

> *The great Queen will see herself*
> *conquered. . . . She will pass over the*
> *river pursued by the sword.*
> *She will have outraged her faith.*

Another oedipal theme reigns supreme. The great Queen is the mother conquered by the sword—the phallic symbol of illicit desire and its dire consequences. Passing over the river signifies that the Queen was made orgasmic by the lusty phallus, or vice versa.

In a quatrain that is said to have foreseen the assassination of President John F. Kennedy in Dallas, Texas, and the uncertainty surrounding the true killer, Nostradamus writes:

> *The ancient work will be accomplished,*
> *And from the roof evil ruin will fall on the great man.*
> *Being dead, they accuse an innocent of the deed:*
> *the guilty one is hidden in the misty woods.*

While seeming spot on, the prophetic element may only be coincidental in that another interpretation of meaning is to be found. As the practice of medicine is an ancient work, the quatrain refers to Nostradamus at a time in his life when he had returned home from curing wealthy patients of the plague. He found evil ruin under his own roof—his wife and children dying from the plague. "Being dead" refers to his family, who could not exonerate Nostradamus, the innocent accused of the deed.

Nostradamus was vilified by his wife's parents, who demanded the return of their daughter's dowry. Refusing their demand, he was taken to court. Worse, his patients deserted him, and he was later charged with heresy and instructed to stand trial before the Church Inquisitor. Thus, he fled ("hidden" from the Inquisitors) in the wooded darkness, leading his mule toward Italy. The guilty one hidden in the misty woods is none other than Nostradamus, succumbing to guilt feelings even though he was an innocent. Indeed, ruin has befallen the great man.

What my analysis reveals is the suggestiveness of symbolic material, in that it is open to varied interpretations. This, however, should not detract from Nostradamus' ability to prophesy, as most of his quatrains remain uncanny in their foresight.

HOW EMPATHY IMPACTS ON PROPHESY

Empathic spirit may have a profound impact on prophesy (see the dream of F.C.D.L.T. in Chapter 16), in that one's personal situation may contribute to one's ability to tap into another impersonal situation of a similar kind. For example, Nostradamus, like President Kennedy, perceived himself to be a great man who fell—not by an assassin's bullet but rather by the assassination of his reputation as a medical doctor, loving husband, and father. In both cases, an innocent is accused. Thus, there is kinship with Oswald. There is also the relationship of Nostradamus losing his wife and children to Jacqueline Kennedy losing her husband and her children losing their father.

There is also the alphabetical similarity of the initials of J. K. (John Kennedy) and M. N. (Michel Nostradamus) as they follow one behind the other. These various similarities, when combined with Nostradamus' theory that the present time exists alongside of the future, may enable a prophetic thought to occur as easily as reaching across the dinner table for some salad. In other words, the past and the future may exist in the same time but in a different space—nonlinear, but simultaneously within grasp.

11

John's
Revelation

t is recorded in the Bible that John is given a prophetic vision or visionary dream of what will come to pass by an angel of Jesus Christ. Interestingly, we will see that John's Revelation is similar to the visions of Ezekiel in that it also prophesies war—perhaps even World War I! Euphemistically adding the groundwork to Ezekiel's vision of a massive air campaign are the symbols of a ground or land attack by tanks that yield an invasive earthly destruction. In Revelation 8:13, the angel warns of disaster: "Woe; woe, woe to the inhabitants of the earth."

The dream interpretation given below involves only those sections of the Revelation that bear resemblance to Ezekiel's visionary dream of war and aviation thousands of years before the fact. An abridged account of John's Revelation follows:

Then out of the smoke locusts came upon the earth. And to them was given power, as the scorpions of the earth have power. . . . They were commanded not to

harm the grass of the earth, or any green thing, or any
tree, but only those men who do not have the seal of
God on their foreheads. 9:3–4

As locusts are powerful, winged, destructive killers that
eat away at the earth, they are viewed as military bombers on
a raid, coming out of the smoky camouflage of the sky.
Having power is an allusion to having power over the air, and
that which is strategic to achieving victory. The scorpions are
the tanks, the war machines that chew up the earth with the
huge treads of their tires. They are commanded to destroy the
enemy, who can be recognized by a visual sign—the color of
its specific uniform. These are the unjust, warring ones,
without the seal of approval.

And the shape of the locusts was like horses prepared
for battle and on their heads were crowns of something
like gold, and their faces were like the faces of men. 9:7

The locusts are compared to horses prepared for battle in
that energy has always been compared to horse power. The
crowns of gold on their heads refer once again to the face of
the plane. The gold is the light shining off the metal of the
plane.

And they had breastplates like breastplates of iron, and
the sound of their wings was like the sound of chariots
with many horses running into battle. . . . They had
tails like scorpions, and there were stings in their tails.
And their power was to hurt men five months. 9:9–10

The breastplates of iron refer to the body of the planes. The
sound of their wings symbolizes the roaring of the engines.

The stings in the tails are either the bombs that fall from the sky to the earth or refer to the previously mentioned symbol of the tanks of war, as the scorpion is a land animal. The tanks shoot out from what could appear to the untrained eye as the tail of a beast. What is released is like a scorpion's poison in that it stings the earth.

> *One woe is past. Behold, still two more woes are coming after these things. 9:12*

Unfortunately, in that there are three woes, the first woe that is past (and specifically mentioned as one woe or woe number one) may refer to World War I, with the other two more woes signifying World War II and possibly World War III. Eerily, the way the sentence is worded, by placing two more woes after the first—woe woe woe—one almost hears "World War One." Scary stuff! Yet if we examine the entire revelation of John, we understand that it is more than anything else a wakeful dream of prophetic warning to mankind.

PART IV

**Examples of
Four Types
of Prophetic
Dreams**

12

The Realistic
Dream

The realistic dream can assume both an active and a passive form. The active form contains subconscious perceptions (intuitive information) that are sensed (but not apprehended during consciousness) and are expressed through movement and activity, symbols, and images. The passive form is stripped bare of any concrete imagery (although a light often appears), perhaps overwhelmed by the awesome presence of a voice that brings a message or warning.

Most realistic dreams are of the passive form, in which the information conveyed is not disguised but rather presented clearly without unconscious elaboration, usually through a clear vocal message. Some realistic dreams, however, are of the active form, in which symbolism is paired with a vocal and physical presence. The following is an example of an active realistic dream that was dreamt in 1779 by **Lord Lyttleton**, of the House of Lords, as recounted by Lord Westcote, uncle to Lord Lyttleton:

*On Thursday the 25th of November, 1779, Thomas
Lord Lyttleton, when he came to breakfast declared ...
that he had an extraordinary dream the night before.
He said he thought he was in a room which a bird flew
into, which appearance was suddenly changed into
that of a woman dressed in white, who bade him prepare to die, to which he answered "I hope not soon, not
in two months." She replied: "Yes, in three days."*

*Apparently Lyttleton did not pay much regard to his
ominous dream because he thought he could account
for some of the symbolism—a few days earlier he had
seen a Robin Redbreast fly into the room of a female
friend, Mrs. Dawson. That day at the House of Lords,
he was heard to say that he did not look as if he was
likely to die. In the evening of the following day, he
said. . . , "I have lived two days and, God willing, I will
live out the third." Saturday morning he told the same
people that he was very well, and "believ'd he should
bilk the ghost." Soon after eleven o'clock at night he
withdrew to his bedchamber, talked cheerfully to his
servant, and stepped into bed with his waistcoat on. As
his servant was removing the garment, Lyttleton put
his hand to his side, sank back, and immediately ex-
pired without a groan.*

Certain dream symbols occur at critical life stages—the
bird is one of them. The bird as a symbol of transcendence is
often used to reflect the emergence of the unconscious as it
enters consciousness. As the room symbolizes the dreamer,
the bird incorporates into his being as a means of expressing
his unconscious contents: his wish to leave the heaviness of
the body, to fly off and become a part of the universe, to ele-
vate, or transcend.

Although unspecified, the bird that flies into the room indicates the presence of an open window. The symbol of the unstated but nevertheless prevalent open window is viewed as the mirror of the soul, yet it may also symbolize one's breathing space in somatic terms (see the dream of Descartes in Chapter 16). The change or transformation of the bird into a woman dressed in white signifies physical transformation of spirit and form and the need for liberation.

Interestingly, the dreamer believed the antecedent of his strange dream was the Robin Redbreast that had flown several days earlier into the room of his married female friend. Thus, we may assume that, although unmentioned, the color of the bird that flew into Lord Lyttleton's room should have been red as well. In that the color of the bird was not stated, the dreamer may have intentionally changed red into white. Going from red to white symbolizes the coldness and stillness of one's life blood and indicates that the unconscious had clear understanding of an existing somatic condition of the dreamer.

The color red is associated with the heart, and the Red Breast is a representation of an enlarged heart. The flapping of bird wings is a symbol of palpitation. The fearful imagery, along with the ominous vocal message from the woman in white, must have brought repression into play. Yet there is another more delicate reason for the deliberate omission of the bird's color. The Red Breast signifies a body part the dreamer may have found uncomfortable to behold in the privacy of his room, as the bird-turned-woman may be none other than the married Mrs. Dawson.

It is unfortunate that the uncle of Lord Lyttleton did not inform us of the cause of death. In that the breathing space or window within Lyttleton's dream is what gives up the ghost, Lyttleton's death may have involved a lax respiratory or circulatory system, which would have contributed to congestive heart failure.

A passive form of realistic dream is exemplified in Pierre Salinger's nocturnal reverie, as related in the Foreword, in that his dreaming unconscious is completely barren of imagery—the dream is heard rather than seen. Unlike Lyttleton's dream, in which the voice takes on shape and form, Pierre's vocal messenger bears no physical presence.

13

The Unrealistic Dream

The unrealistic dream presents information in disguised, encoded, or veiled symbolic form, in which a message is unclear. For example, the message may be represented by a parallel situation, such as the biblical story of Pharaoh, who dreamt of "seven fat kine (cattle) and seven lean kine." The images are often convoluted and difficult to recognize. The scenes may shift. In brief, these dreams are often misinterpreted because, although there is imagery present, it is usually inappropriate to the dreamer's present situation and thus unrealistic in terms of believability. In addition, upon speculation there is no accountable daytime residue or antecedent to the dream.

Having imagery and symbolism, the dreams are of active form, wherein the dreamer often participates in the dream, as opposed to being an impassive observer. The following is an example of an active, unrealistic dream that was dreamt by **Percy Bysshe Shelley** on June 24, 1822, two weeks before his death on July 7, as recounted by Mary Shelley:

He said that he had not been asleep, and that it was a vision that he saw that had frightened him. But as he declared that he had not screamed, it was certainly a dream, and no waking vision. What had frightened him was this. He dreamt that, lying as he did in bed, Edward and Jane [Williams] came in to him; they were in the most horrible condition; their bodies lacerated, the bones starting through their skin, their faces pale yet stained with blood; they could hardly walk, but Edward was the weakest, and Jane supporting him. Edward said, "Get up, Shelley, the sea is flooding the house, and it is all coming down." Shelley got up, he thought, and went to his window that looked on the terrace and the sea, and thought he saw the sea rushing in. Suddenly his vision changed, and he saw the figure of himself strangling me; that made him rush into my room, yet, fearful of frightening me, he dared not approach the bed, when my jumping out awoke him, or as he phrased it, caused his vision to vanish.

The first part of Shelley's dream is translucent in its tragic imagery but only in retrospect, as it clearly holds the unconscious knowledge of Shelley's drowning. When Edward (a friend who later drowns with Shelley) and his wife Jane come into Shelley's room, he incorporates them into his psyche or persona. The fact that they are in a most horrible condition suggests that Shelley himself may have been emotionally depressed at the time of the dream. (The sea that threatens to engulf the house represents the unconscious, and an escape into it, a means to submerge or avoid reality). The lacerations of the body reflect that something from inside is coming out—the bones and blood pour out, as the body can no longer hold them. Similarly, the sea that floods the house is not contained within its normal confines or physical boundaries. The sea that will engulf the house is interpreted as the overwhelming of the dreamer by an outside source. His house or self coming down by the weight of the sea is a prophetic allusion to the immediate future drowning or flooding of his lungs.

The pale-faced friends represent death and the shock of one's death (Edward dies, leaving his wife Jane pale with grief).

The second part of Shelley's dream is more complex, as the defensive process of transference is at work. The frightful thought of himself being brought down by the sea, gasping for air, is so horrific that it necessitates an attempt at transference, wherein Mary becomes the recipient of choice of the Neptunian onslaught—the one who is strangled instead of Shelley, so that she may do the choking.

Even unconsciously, Shelley is aware that he dare not approach the bed or supporting structure of his malevolent wish—that Mary be sacrificed or given over to death as a substitute victim.

Two weeks after the dream, Percy Bysshe Shelley and Edward Williams were drowned in a storm, on the Bay of Spezia on July 7, 1822. It is said that Shelley would not comply with Williams' demands to bring the boat in.

14

The Realistic and the Unrealistic Dream Combined

The third kind of prophetic dream contains both realistic and unrealistic elements (see Jeane Dixon's dream of her brother, and her dream of Joe Kennedy and Job, in Chapter 19). In other words, the message or prophetic information contained within the dream is partly disguised, encoded, or symbolically veiled and unclear, yet is partly recognizable. Often the vocal part of the dream will be clear, leaving the narrative of symbols and images in a vague or ambiguous state.

The following is an example of a symbolic vision that contains realistic and unrealistic elements. It was dreamt by **Saint Francis of Assisi** as recounted by the Chronicler, Matthew of Pais. (Note: I have transformed the dream into the first person.)

On his way to be knighted, Francis was about to join the papal armies led by the Norman captain Gautier de Brienne in the service of Pope Innocent III:

My father's house changed into a marvelous palace filled with arms. The bales of cloth had disappeared, and were replaced by magnificent saddles, shields, lances, and all kinds of knightly harness. Moreover, in one room of the palace a beautiful and charming bride was waiting for her bridegroom. . . . Then a voice revealed to me that the soldiers and this beautiful lady were reserved for me.

Francis, who was not yet sainted, interpreted his dream as symbolic of the success he was to achieve as a knight. But as time went by and his marvelous dream (encoded as it was) did not come to pass, Francis became despondent, realizing that he had made an incorrect interpretation.

An interpretation suggests the following: The symbol of his father's house is a religious metaphor for heaven; more interesting is that the house is representative of Francis himself. Thus, the dream relates that the kingdom of heaven is already within Francis. The house that changed represents the transformation within Francis that is yet to come—the conversion—in expiation of his former lifestyle of frivolous fault and irresponsible excesses. The arms that fill the palace represent the charity of alms (in its universal symbol) and of giving.

Yet Francis' dream reveals him to be too much in the world of the material, wishing for "saddles, shields, lances and all kinds of knightly harness." Yet, as the lance symbolizes the penetrating function of the intellect, perhaps the bales of cloth that disappear signify that a veil has been lifted to reveal, as it were, the weaponry of possessions that defend against an ascetic life, as they are what "harness" or restrain the knight from becoming a vassal of Christ—and what must be given up.

The bride who waits for her bridegroom represents a spiritual union that occurs in the future. Six years after Francis' conversion, he established the order of Poor Ladies, with Saint Clare (Lady Poverty) as the princess he hoped to wed. Thus Francis' dream reveals his gain of a different kind of glory.

Some time later, during an evening stopover at Spoleto, Francis heard the same voice of his former dream. The voice questioned him in his sleep:

> *"Francis, where are you going like this?" to which he responded, "I am going to fight in Apulia." The voice continued, "Tell me, from whom can you expect the most, the master or the servant?" Francis replied, "From the master, of course." Then the voice questioned him again, "Then why follow the servant, instead of the master on whom he depends?" At this point Francis must have realized the divine presence and addressed God, "Lord, what would you have me do?" The Lord answered Francis, "Return to your own country. Then it shall be revealed to you what you are to do, and you will come to understand the meaning of this vision."*

The first question involves Francis' sense of direction and reflects his own anxiety over indecision. This is his inner voice of reason questioning his motives and signifies internal conflict. Heeding the voice of his dream, Francis returned home to Assisi, with his faith surpassing doubt. Soon his prophetic dream of becoming a knight became a reality in that his soul transcended from indifference to fervor and mystical love. Indeed, he became another sort of knight, shining from the glorious light of God.

15

The Vision

The fourth type of prophetic dream is the vision or wakeful dream (see Chapter 9, Vision as Wakeful Dream). The wakeful dream occurs when the subject has a reverie that intersects consciousness midway between preconsciousness and the unconscious. The dream or vision is seen or viewed through open eyes. The viewer or one who envisions is undisturbed by worldly stimuli.

The vision is passive when the viewer is a silent listener, active when there is conversation between the viewer and the divine exterior voice. Sometimes the vision is as still as a silent movie—a picture may superimpose itself on the surroundings and block out everything else. Jeane Dixon was in St. Matthew's Cathedral, in front of the statue of the Virgin Mary, when the White House suddenly popped into view. An ominous dark cloud encroached upon the building. A young man with a shock of thick brown hair stood in front of the main door with his hands at his side. The numbers 1-9-6-0 briefly covered the sky. The vision itself, although filled with realistic details, would have appeared unrealistic and extremely difficult for Jeane to interpret if she had not heard an explanatory voice tell her its meaning. The voice instructed that the man, a Democrat, would be seated as President, but would be assassinated and would die in office (see Chapter 19, on Jeane Dixon).

Another vision was experienced by a young man who was riding the subway. He told me that during the time of the vision his concentration was intense. He would not have noticed if the train had stopped at his station. He would have remained in his seat until the vision faded away, almost as if he was a captive audience. Ironically and in retrospect, it seems that he was given an audience with a higher power. His vision follows:

I was sitting down when suddenly I saw the evening sky obliterating every other view. I saw many stars. The stars arranged themselves in the heavens into the shape of the number seventeen. In actuality, there were seventeen stars as I counted them. I knew the number seventeen was extremely important. Then I heard a loud noise as though something had ruptured. I had this vision before the seventeenth of the month. On the seventeenth Kobe in Japan had a major earthquake.

How is it possible that this train rider was able to see into the future and predict (had he tried to interpret his vision before the fact) the tragic earthquake that befell Japan? Perhaps he had hooked into the Akashic Records—a storage place of all past, present, and future information. The mystics and spiritualists believe the Akashic Records is what the Bible refers to as the Book of Life or the Book of All Days.

As the vision was unrealistic and non-interpretable to the

viewer's perspective, one wonders why it was given at all. Was the vision nothing more than a coincidence? At best, the computation of numbers within the vision signifies the dreamer's connection between the material world and that of his psyche. At a theoretical impasse like this, perhaps asking the right question is more important than receiving the right answer!

PART V

**Three
Prophesy
Dream Motifs
and
Dream
Analyses**

16

Prophetic Warning Dreams: Dreams That Predict Death, Illness, or Physical Harm

As Edgar Cayce would agree (see Chapter 20), it seems that our unconscious minds, and therefore our dreams in particular, are the *cognoscenti* of our existence, in that the unconscious knows everything there is to know about us. More intriguingly, it appears that the unconscious mind busies itself in assessing our personalities, our behaviors, our actions, and our needs, and that, on the basis of this personal information, it determines what the rest of our lives have in store for us. This is the predictive value of dreams. If we are to learn what the future holds, we must scrutinize dreams with the intention of decoding the encrypted symbolism and imagery in what may be a defensive, last-ditch attempt to save our hides. We need to interpret dreams to determine where the joker is hiding, just as a deck must be spread to see how the cards are stacked.

Even though Freud, as we shall see, was not a believer in prophetic dreams, there is reason to believe that he would have been in agreement with Cayce's basic premise: Dreams are created from our individually perceived conscious material and therefore may have far-reaching predictive implications. When Freud is presented with a dream that is believed to be prophetic, he interprets it as something that is at one point in time consciously thought and wished for. In other words, Freud believes that a dream merely re-creates former conscious thoughts. He does, however, acknowledge that numerous parallels may be drawn between dream-life and preexisting unknown conditions of psychical illness in waking life. For example, an undiagnosed schizophrenic dream of a tree that is sliced in half as it is struck by lightning; the dream is prophetic in that the unconscious knows something before consciousness does, and it is predictive in that it cites evidence of destructive disorganization.

Freud was given the following dream of **Descartes** along with Descartes' self-analysis of his dream. Yet, because Freud does not buy into the idea that dreams make predictive pronouncements of the future, he overlooks somatic symbolism that is crucial to a prophetic understanding. The dream appears to prognosticate a physiological weakness and a future ailment that causes Descartes' death thirty years later.

The following prophetic dream of Descartes (transcribed into the first person) was dreamt in 1620 or thereabouts, and reveals how he will die:

> *All was fever, thunderstorms, panic, . . . phantoms rose before me. I tried to get up in order to drive them away, but I fell back, ashamed, feeling troubled by a great weakness in my right side. All at once, a window in the room opened. Terrified, I felt myself carried away by the gusts of a violent wind which made me whirl round several times on my left foot. Dragging myself, stag-*

gering along, I reached the buildings of the college in which I had been educated. I tried desperately to enter the chapel, to make my devotions. At that moment some people passed by. I wanted to stop in order to speak with them; I noticed that one of them was carrying a melon. But a violent wind drove me back toward the chapel. [Then] I awakened with twinges of sharp pain in my left side.

There is no doubt that the twinges of sharp pain Descartes feels in his left side upon waking have filtered into his dream, as a somatic cause often produces a dream reaction. An actual physical weakness is present, and the pain is experienced as a great weakness. Yet the dream produces a corrective alternative: Within the dream, the weakness is experienced in the right side of the dreamer as opposed to the left, indicating perhaps that the dream as a whole is trying to right or correct the situation. Overlooking the somatic verity of Descartes' pain and the historical truth of the dream (Descartes died of pneumonia in 1650), Freud interprets this weakness in the following manner: Descartes feels that he has sinned and therefore his left side is stronger.

However, in that a room—a walled-in, interior space—symbolizes the person, the physical or mental condition of the dreamer may be assessed. The fever, thunderstorms, panic, and phantoms that rise within the room reveal the inner physical turmoil of the dreamer, as these are somatically induced images. The sense of these images or feelings rising may actually represent the rising and falling of the lobes of the lungs, especially when examined together and in context with the symbol of the window in the room that opens, for the window is the breathing space that signifies the lungs.

But the window has another symbolic meaning: It may also represent the door of the soul, or the door to the future. What is clear is that the dreamer, by his own words, is terrified of being carried away by the gusts of a violent wind. A storm of passion perhaps or a frightening prophesy curiously makes the dreamer unstable as he whirls round several times on his left foot, a symbol that may be interpreted as meaning that the dreamer has only one leg left to stand on, as the other is in the grave already.

Dragging himself along, the dreamer desperately tries to enter a chapel to make his devotions, which has the significance of prayerful rites. Once outside, Descartes notices people passing by; one in particular is carrying a melon. The melon bears most interest, for therein lies a significant clue to the prophetic nature of the dream. Freud writes that the melon "must remain unexplained," even though Descartes openly interprets the melon as having the "charms of solitude" ("melon" is quite similar to the French word *mélancolie*). Freud was critical of Descartes' judgment, saying, "This is certainly not correct." One thing is certain: The melon is a wish-induced symbol, as Descartes has put it there himself with a distinct purpose in mind. In that Descartes knew the Greek language, and in that the Greek word for "the future" is *to mellon*, it is likely that Descartes wished to be presented with the future or a prophetic vision of things to come.

Reinforcing this interpretation is another dream of Descartes from the same night (also transcribed in the first person). Any dream that follows close upon another must be considered as a thematic continuation, especially when the dreamer himself connects it as such. Descartes prefaced the telling of the dream by referring yet again to the self-same fever and pain that he experienced in the first dream. He spoke of having dreamed again "with [his] brain on fire, excited by vague sufferings." Of this dream, Descartes wrote that it specifically changes his ideas. Descartes' dream made a profound and lasting impact on his ideology to the degree that the dream is indeed ideationally predictive: He linked science (as symbolized by a dictionary) with philosophy (as symbolized by a collection of poems). He believed that the following dream proved that observational scientific reasoning should be applied to any matter of philosophic inquiry:

> *I opened a dictionary and a collection of poems. I read the line* "Quod vitae sectabor iter? *(What path in life shall I follow?)."* *Then, suddenly, there appeared a man I did not know, who intended to make me read a passage from Ausonius beginning with the words* "Est et non *(It is and is not)."* *But the man disappeared, and another took his place. The book vanished in its turn, then reappeared decorated with portraits in copperplate. Finally the night drew quiet.*

The very act of opening a dictionary is symbolic of the dreamer's quest for knowledge. What is read in the book of poems ("What path in life shall I follow?") manifests the dreamer's uncertainty, his wish for prophetic wisdom, and firmly establishes that the dream is concerned with the future. The passage from Ausonius—"It is and is not"—is esoteric and mystical, as it questions the matter of being, of truth and falsehood. Perhaps Descartes is pondering whether his dream is real or not, or whether it is a prophesy. The book that vanishes in the past and reappears in the future is the book of answers, as it is timeless. The book reappears decorated with portraits in copperplate. This necessarily means that the portraits or remembrances are etched, as etching is the only way that portraits may be drawn in copperplate. Thus the portraits appear in a medium or form that cannot change or be altered, as this is Descartes' destiny. Assured of his immortality, of his place in history, Descartes can rest in peace, which is why "the night grows quiet."

It seems that **President Abraham Lincoln** was more than just a great president; it turns out that "Honest Abe" was a prophet as well. Lincoln had been up "very late," as he was "waiting for important dispatches from the front." Being "weary," he fell into a slumber and dreamt the following uncanny dream shortly before he was assassinated:

There seemed to be death-like stillness about me. Then I heard subdued sobs, as if a number of people were weeping. I thought I left my bed and wandered downstairs. There the silence was broken by the same pitiful sobbing, but the mourners were invisible. I went from room to room; no living person was in sight, but the same mournful sounds of distress met me as I passed along. It was light in all the rooms; every object was familiar to me; but where were all the people who were grieving as if their hearts would break? I was puzzled and alarmed. What could be the meaning of all this? Determined to find the cause of a state of things so mysterious and so shocking, I kept on until I arrived at the East Room, which I entered. There I met with a sickening surprise. Before me was a catafalque, on which rested a corpse wrapped in funeral vestments. Around it were stationed soldiers who were acting as guards; and there was a throng of people, some gazing mournfully upon the corpse, whose face was covered, others weeping pitifully. "Who is dead in the White House?" I demanded of one of the soldiers. "The President" was his answer; "he was killed by an assassin!" Then came a loud burst of grief from the crowd, which awoke me from my dream. (Ward Hill Lamon, Recollections of Abraham Lincoln, 1847–1855*)*

Lincoln's conscious effort of waiting for dispatches from the front may have unconsciously translated into his wanting to know what is happening up ahead and sets the scene for a prophetic dream. Leaving the bed signifies the willful determination of the dreamer to be active, independent, and definitely vital. The image of wandering downstairs refers to the President's quest to reach a deeper level of conscious awareness, as downstairs is underneath and represents the unconscious. Going from room to room symbolizes a thorough search of his personality, his being. He is suffering someplace within himself, but his suffering does not permit pity.

There is light in all the rooms because there is a revelation: a cry of distress, of puzzlement and alarm. The dreamer's determination to find the cause of such a mysterious state of affairs shows an analytic mind. As the sun rises in the east, the answer *dawns* on the President in the East Room: The President is dead, having been killed by an assassin. In a psychoanalytic view, being dead in the White House is a self-referential recrimination and even condemnation of a *weary* President who feels guilty about falling asleep on the nation. Perhaps he feels that he is too old for the job, that he is already a corpse. From a paranormal standpoint, the dream is nothing but prophetic.

The following prophetic dream was dreamt by **Pierre Salinger**, former press secretary to President John F. Kennedy:

In August 1982, I was on vacation in Corsica for one month when I dreamt I heard in my brain the words "You should be aware that one of the worst terrorist attacks will take place in Paris, in August, in the last week." I left for Paris immediately, and the day after I arrived a bomb exploded in a Jewish restaurant.

Having just been working with ABC covering terrorism, Mr. Salinger's dream may be viewed as a measure of his conscientiousness, for his dream is deeply committed and connected to his work of the moment. Even on vacation, he cannot let down his guard. Thus, Mr. Salinger's dream commands that he should be aware of the evils of society; the dream gives the warning to be wary. But, interestingly, in that Mr. Salinger is half-French, the dream may reflect a recognition of some personal turmoil or upheaval, in which the city of Paris may symbolize the dreamer himself. In other words, if a difficult situation is not dealt with, it will become explosive.

The prophetic nature of Pierre's dream cannot be discounted, as the dream's prediction actually occurred—in late August 1982 a bomb blew up a small Jewish bakery in Paris. The dream must therefore be viewed as a measure of Mr. Salinger's sensitive and intuitive nature, although, because of the specific biblical manner in which the prophesy was worded, one wonders if the prophesy was referring to something far worse than the 1982 terrorist attack, to something more horrific that has not yet happened.

Worded in biblical fashion, the phrase "in the last week" brings biblical significance to the dream; a "week" would be interpreted as seven years, and the "last week" would allude to the end of all days or Armageddon. The dream would take on a darker perspective as the "worst terrorist" would be symbolically euphemistic for the ultimate biblical demon, Satan.

What is absolutely extraordinary about Mr. Salinger's prophetic dream is the time frame within which it was told. Pierre first told me this dream at 2:00 P.M. on August 30, 1997—just hours before an unspeakable tragedy occurred "in Paris, in August, in the last week": the fatal car crash of Princess Diana and her companion, Dodi Al Fayed. Indeed, had not the frenzied pack of paparazzi, in hot pursuit, "terrorized" the car that desperately tried to speed away?

Adding to the strangeness of Pierre choosing to tell me his dream on the last day of August (I had been waiting several months for him to call me with his dream), during the exact period of time that the dream warns about, is the fact that four hours later I faxed Pierre's interpreted dream to my friend Soheir Khashoggi, who was about to fax me a dream of her own to look at. Soheir is the aunt of Dodi Al Fayed. I cannot imagine what provoked me to fax Soheir this particular dream of Pierre's as I had more than two hundred dreams to choose from. An eerie coincidence or a fateful communication? The latter case would signify that Soheir Khashoggi was meant to know that her nephew's car crash was no accident.

The following telepathic dream was dreamt in Connecticut the morning of June 6, 1968, at approximately 4:43 A.M., moments before Robert F. Kennedy was pronounced dead at 1:44 A.M. Pacific Time, and therefore during the exact time of the assassination. The dream belongs to the first cousin of Jacqueline Bouvier Kennedy, **John Davis**:

I was being engulfed in an ocean of excrement or human sewage. It was falling down from the sky like rain and I was drowning in it. I knew something horrible, something catastrophic had happened, but I was unsure of what it was.

Prominent author John Davis had been up late that night working on a chapter from his forthcoming book, *The Bouviers: From Waterloo to the Kennedys and Beyond.* Ironically, the chapter discusses Bobby Kennedy's candidacy for the Presidency and envisions the possible restoration of John F. Kennedy's spirit in the White House.

Considering the task at hand and the familial relationship of Mr. Davis to President Kennedy, there may be a fair amount of the empathic in the telepathic. I use the word "telepathic" because John Davis seems to have picked up his premonitory thoughts simultaneously with the occurrence of the event. In other words, the dream does not come to pass— *the dream is during the passing!*

It must be noted that John Davis had been filled with grim apprehension upon the announcement of R.F.K.'s candidacy. But in that he awoke from his gruesome presentiment one minute before R.F.K. was declared dead, it is entirely reasonable to view this dream as more than just a condemnation of a corrupt and corrosive society, as it appears to be one of deep telepathic nature.

In Revelation 8:10 the Bible refers to "a great star [that] fell from heaven, burning like a torch, on a third of the rivers" as being a symbol of foreboding destruction. Similarly, when a dream reveals something ominous coming from above, falling down from the sky, it is usually viewed as a warning signal. Whereas rain is a birth symbol of nourishment, survival, and purification, the raining of excrement or human sewage is its horrific opposite—a death symbol of decay, defilement, and putrefaction.

The ocean, which symbolizes a birth vision, becomes an ocean of excrement and represents a deathly vision. Excrement is a symbolic image that evokes being defiled. It engulfs the dreamer and/or R.F.K.; it is aurally similar to the word "execution." The image of human sewage identifies the source of this defilement of life as coming from humankind; this was painfully evidenced in both Kennedy killings. The bullets that in reality rained through the air are symbolically linked to the precipitation of defecation.

The core of the dream is a condemnation of uncivilized contemporary society. It warns the dreamer that he must find a way to rise above the human sewage that threatens to drown or engulf respectability and all that is decent in an assassination of unspeakable defilement.

The dream is also strangely prescient of Robert Kennedy, Jr.'s current environmental concerns. The raining of human defecation refers to man's destructive pollution of the world around him—the oceans, the atmosphere, and the rain forest.

On the day and at the exact time that Elvis Presley died, **Larry Geller,** hair stylist, friend, and spiritual mentor of Elvis, had the following telepathic dream:

At the exact time Elvis was dying, I dreamt a horrific nightmare that a groaning monster, a monstrous eight-foot gorilla, was chasing me. Every time its claws got close to me I got away. Then I saw Elvis in the clouds, his arms reaching out to help me, and I levitated up from the ground away from this monster.

Dreams that involve being chased indicate that the dreamer feels grounded in a life situation, but more importantly often symbolize the phonetic meaning of *chaste*; this establishes that the dreamer is of high moral and ethical sensibility. Thus, the dream contains the wish for justification and self-affirmation, and ultimately the wish to be lifted from the darkness.

The nightmarish claws of the monster figuratively represent that someone wants a piece of the dreamer. But redemption follows in the symbol of a risen Elvis whose arms or "alms" (in a phonetic sense) lovingly lift Larry beyond his worldly problems. The levitation is the wish to rise above the heaviness of the moment. Larry has to run away from those members of Presley's entourage who, in the past, have resented Larry's profound influence over and close bond with his friend Elvis.

Viewed as prophetic and prescient, the dream reveals Larry's empathic connection to his friend's personal torment and suffering—his timely (telepathic) understanding and perception of Elvis's sense of being driven. For on this level of interpretation, Elvis is the one who is pursued by his own engorged and monstrous being, with death as his only escape from his personal heaviness, both physical and emotional, into the weightlessness of clouds. In symbolic identification, Larry is Elvis running away from himself. This substitution of self reveals the immense bond and connection the dreamer has with his friend.

The levitation represents the transformation from the material world to the realm of the metaphysical. Thus, the spiritual content of the dream suggests that Larry has visualized Elvis as both rescuer (savior) and one who is rescued (resurrected), and establishes the wishful belief that Elvis, watching from above, will always be there for him and for those who are in need. The heavenly image of Elvis in the clouds suggests that the dreamer's unconscious already knows or perceives that Elvis is no longer among the living.

☽

The following prophetic dream was dreamt by the artist **Ron Ferri** about our mutual friend, Ludovic Autet (see the account of Ludovic's prophetic dream, below) on the day that Ludovic passed away:

> *In my sleep my friend called me. I didn't pick up; the answering machine did. He sounded like he wanted someone to talk to—like calling for help. I got up at 7 A.M. to check my machine, but there was no message. At 10 P.M. that night I was informed that my friend had passed away hours after I had walked him home.*

In that Ron had just spent Thanksgiving with the self-same friend who appears in his dream, the friend he had just walked home at 5:00 A.M., the dream indicates that Ron must have intuitively sensed something wrong about this friend that worried him. He may have sensed that his friend needed help in some way. Yet, whereas the lateness of the hour made a talk unrealistic, the dream fulfilled Ron's wish for a renewed communication with his friend, as the friend calls Ron within the dream.

The phrase "I didn't pick up" symbolizes that the dreamer is chastising himself for neither understanding the situation consciously nor acting on his instincts. Ron does not delve into his prophetic ruminations, but rather allows a non-sentient machine to receive the intuitive communication.

Interestingly, the telephone usually symbolizes a device that communicates with the dead, as it is a receiver that connects a voice to the other side, to distant invisible voices from far away. As Ron's friend actually dies later on in the day, his dream is considered one of precognition, as the death event is perceived shortly before it occurs.

))

In an earlier interpretation in which I have referred to this dream as one of initiation, it now seems clear that the dream has prophetic value. Of particular significance is the fact that Ludovic's dream was dreamt a year before his massive heart attack and premature death at fifty. The dream itself reveals Ludovic's strong intuitive wisdom, as the dream foreshadows his ultimate initiation into the hereafter. World-renowned jeweler Ronald Winston has referred to Ludovic as "Harry Winston's ambassador to the stars." Here follows the prophetic dream of my beloved friend, the social arbitor and bon vivant **Ludovic Autet**:

> *I dreamt I was in my bedroom when suddenly from a long hall I saw two dogs coming toward my room, one yellow, the other black. I shut my door, but somehow the dark dog came through the door and got into my bedroom. It looked menacing, like a panther, but when it climbed onto my bed I embraced it, and we lay embracing, sleeping.*

In Ludovic's mystical dream the unconscious advances in the shape of a black dog that thrusts itself upon the scene, going through a closed door. This symbolizes the powerful, intellectual, and moral effort needed to examine this dark, closed-off, evening side of our psyche. The door, an entrance into the unknown, is always frightening. But, in heroic style, Ludovic confronts the aggressor on his own, seeking no external help from the yellow dog outside the door, which represents the light of day, a safe entity. Embracing the menacing dog that transforms into a panther reveals Ludovic's fearless love of challenge. In that a dog also symbolizes death, the transformation from dog to panther presents the transformation of the soul into spirit.

Like Sir Galahad searching for the Holy Grail, Ludovic succeeds; he gets in touch with his instincts and soothes the savage beast. That he disarms and tames the menacing panther reveals Ludovic's natural charm, his seductiveness. Ludovic is literally embracing his own death. This prophetic initiation dream signifies that Ludovic is on the verge of enlightenment, for in order to reach the light, one must first go through the darkness of the tunnel! Which he does, ever so beautifully, on November 28, 1997.

The following problem-solving dream dreamt by **Monique van Vooren**, actress, author, singer, and closest friend of Rudolf Nureyev, is also prophetic in that it was dreamt well in advance of Nureyev's sickness, his bed-ridden condition, his physical deterioration, and eventual death:

> *I went to a house that was dilapidated. It was scary. To enter the house there were many rickety stairs. But when I entered the door the hallway was luxurious, beautiful, and the lighting was low. On the floor there were the lines of chalk that the police draw to indicate a body was there, and a harsh light was on that spot. Someone had been killed, and I ran upstairs to a room, and Rudolf Nureyev was in this room. He was in a crib, tied up.*

This dream reflects the deep concern that the dreamer has for her close friend Rudolf Nureyev; it imaginatively comes up with a solution to save him from harm's way. Concern for his well-being is shown by the dreamer visualizing him tied up in a crib, for a crib represents a safety zone. Similarly, the crib symbolizes the dreamer's wish to protect Nureyev in motherly fashion from a perceived danger, in that the chalk lines at the bottom of the stairs indicate that death is close by. The harsh light highlighting those ominous lines of chalk is the stark, harsh reality of her friend's private lifestyle, being promiscuous in the era of AIDS.

In that houses in dreams represent the body, a dilapidated, run-down exterior can represent the wearing away of one's physical being through disease. Although somewhat afraid, Monique bravely enters the door and finds that the interior (the mind, the soul of her friend) is still luxurious and beautiful.

Whereas climbing up the stairs is the wish for a sexual relationship, within the dream Nureyev can only be possessed and/or loved platonically. The mother, as one who births and cribs, is the rescuer, which allows this dream to be viewed as a rescue fantasy in which the dreamer has to overcome certain fears or hardships. As a house can also symbolize the mind, stepping inside the house symbolizes that the dreamer is looking beyond the surface and making an effort to understand the life inside of the home—the mind and the lifestyle of her friend. And although there is seductiveness ("the lighting was low"), danger is harboring nearby, for someone has been killed.

The image of Nureyev being tied up symbolizes time and means that a delay is hoped for. This symbol also represents the wish that things be under the dreamer's control or dominance, that Nureyev be submissive to her demands; in reality, the dreamer is aware that she cannot stop her friend from that which will inevitably kill him or bring about his demise.

Horse breeder and racer **Davy Jones**, formerly of the rock group The Monkees, had the following childhood prophetic dream:

When I was fourteen I had seen a movie called A Kid for Two Farthings, *about a little white goat with a horn in the middle of its head that a little boy perceived as a unicorn. Some time later I had a dream that there were doctors coming up and down the stairs to my mother. There was this big, big unicorn with wings that came to me and sort of hovered outside the terrace window. I got my mother and got on the unicorn with my mother and we flew off somewhere. (My mother was ill at the time, and died shortly after the dream.)*

This poignantly prophetic wish-fulfillment dream presents an idyllic oedipal fantasy, wherein a young boy is magically enabled to fly off with his mother into a land where anything is possible. Children often have the need to empower themselves in dreams that compensate for their sense of helplessness and dependent existence (particularly when a parent or caretaker is perceived as being ill), and Davy bonds with a unicorn, a symbol of magical power and presence. Yet, whereas the "big, big" unicorn represents the male power and strength of a horse, it also signifies an omnipotent authority in that it is able to fly. Thus, the mythic creature, with its ability to fly, symbolizes the wish to rise above all earthly problems or insecurities and lift the sagging spirits of its rider.

Davy's mother was ill at the time of the dream, and there is the wish to cure her and make her well. Having identified with the unicorn that hovers outside his window (his psyche) the dreamer compensates for his fear of abandonment through death through his newfound ability of transcendence. Davy's unconscious desire is to remain with his mother, even in her flight to the other world or heaven, which reveals his close maternal relationship and his empathic nature.

The doctors coming up and down the stairs represent a sense of urgency, as Davy's mother is already perceived as being on a higher level that can be accessed only by stairs. Interestingly, the occurrence of the mother's death shortly after the dream may indicate the dream's inherent prophetic value, wherein the winged unicorn is viewed as an angel substitute that accompanies Davy's mother on her parting journey, and the stairs are symbolic of the stairway to heaven.

In retrospect, what had seemed a recurring flying dream to actress **Arlene Dahl** was actually a recurring prophetic dream of warning:

> *After an automobile accident I had an out-of-body experience. The doctors could not find a pulse. . . . I was floating high above, looking down at myself on the operating table, watching the doctors prodding me. Prior to the accident I had been having this recurring dream where I was floating high above, flying in the sky, watching people down in the streets, walking, dancing, getting on with their lives. I felt like a spirit that comes in and out through windows.*

Amazingly, Arlene's recurring dream serves as a premonition: It foreshadows the aftereffect of a death-defying event, an auto accident. Arlene's dream produces a similar sensation to that of her actual out-of-body experience—she floats high above and watches what is happening down in the streets. The dream phrase "people getting on with their lives" presupposes that something has happened, something that must be gotten over. But Arlene is not one of the people getting on with life. She is floating in the sky on a higher level, unseen, like a spirit.

Flying dreams express the wish to look at something objectively in that the dreamer is removed from the rest of the world—cool, detached, and with a bird's-eye view. But these dreams also signify the need to get away from it all—to rise above one's problems, which may indicate that in certain cases there is a significant problem that needs to be dealt with.

Floating in the sky symbolizes the need to slow down time, in that the further we are from a situation, the more time we have to deal with it. As the focus of Arlene's dream is watching, the dream may be interpreted as a warning to pay strict attention to what is going on in life.

A year before her friend's death, **Ghislaine** had the following prophetic dream, a dream that prophesied her friend's death and also gave a visual image of how her friend would look in his last days:

I dreamt that my friend was in a tomb underneath a huge cathedral with arcades and columns. There were columns everywhere. Nothing was there but the casket. He came out of it with a white sarong around his waist, very skinny and bony like a skeleton. He came over to me and spit on me. (In reality my friend got sick a year later and died, and he looked exactly like he did in the dream.)

In Ghislaine's prophetic dream, she is visited (in what seems like a visitation dream of the deceased) by her soon-to-be-deceased friend before he is deceased. This raises the following question: Does this predictive knowledge emanate from the pre-deceased via his projected thought into the dreamer's unconscious, or does this information already exist within the unconscious dreamer from what was intuited subliminally during consciousness? Or does this dream represent a random coincidental occurrence?

From a psychoanalytic perspective there are no coincidences. In a psychoanalytic interpretation, the dreamer may well have used a symbol of projection—the spit—to symbolize her own projection. In other words, when the dreamer's friend spits, he becomes a spitting image, a perfect likeness or counterpart of the dreamer herself. Moreover, the act of expectorating means that something internal is being spewed out or ejected externally: The dreamer's buried emotional content rises up from the casket into consciousness. Interestingly, a part of the dreamer that has been enshrined and encased comes out of its concealment, only to be self-vilified by the spit of a friend, who is simultaneously both Ghislaine and her friend, with whom she has a love-hate relationship.

Along this line of reasoning, the friend, viewed as himself, is presented as a Jesus figure (skinny and bony in a white sarong) who resurrects from the casket of death in what should be interpreted as a manifestation of the pure transcendence of spirit. But whereas a beneficent blessing would be in order, the friend angrily judges Ghislaine by spitting at her in what must be considered an innate desire for self-vilification that may follow from her loss of faith in the life of a friendship.

Associated with the loving part of her relationship, the many columns indicate that Ghislaine's wish is, on the one hand, to be supportive of her friend. On the other hand, the hating part manifests itself in non-supportive behavior, in behavior that will bring about self-recrimination and feelings of guilt. The personal guilt of the dreamer is then projected outward onto her friend in the form of spit, wherein the emotion of hate rids itself through having been spit on. The receiver of the spit is no longer the hater but the recipient of the hate.

In a paranormal view, the dreamer's unconscious has connected with the presentiment of her friend's emaciation and forthcoming death from AIDS. Interestingly, the projectile spit, when viewed as the transmission of a bodily fluid, suggests the wish of the dreamer to connect or enjoin with her friend through contagion.

The following prophetic dream was dreamt by **Jack S.** when he was fifteen years old. The year was 1927, and he had been living in San Bruno, California, with his parents in a large house. His mother, never having fully recovered from witnessing the death of her two-year-old child in a train crash the year before in New York City, was taken to a hospital in Napa County for nervous disorders. Jack missed his mother, and it was his habit to lock his bedroom door each night before going to sleep. One night, when he went to sleep, he dreamt a strange and prophetic dream:

I dreamt that my mother had died in the hospital. Attendants were placing her body in a coffin. I saw the coffin being placed in an ambulance. The ambulance was driving to my home. It stopped by my front door. The back doors of the ambulance opened, and the coffin was pulled out. The coffin opened, and my mother got out, still dressed in hospital garments. She walked to the door of my home and turned the knob of the door. My bedroom was on the second floor. I saw her walking up the steps, walking toward my door. She turned the knob, and my door opened wide. She looked at me for what seemed like a long time. She took her hand and ran it over my forehead. (Upon awakening I was

*mystified to see that the door to my room was open just
as in my dream. Some time after my mother came home
from the hospital, my family moved back to New York.
My mother was re-hospitalized and died the following
year, in the hospital.)*

The enclosed, air-tight, boxed-in image of the coffin symbolizes the mother's total confinement; in reality, she is hospitalized and out of sight. The trauma of the mother's
hospitalization is what anxiously leads the young dreamer to
fear that his mother will never come home again. Thus, the
wish of the dreamer is primarily to see his mother again, one
way or another. The dreamer's worst fear is interpreted as
both realized and assuaged. If his mother is to die, it is con-
soling to think that she will still be able to visit and watch
over him in motherly attention. The opening of the coffin an-
nihilates the fear of death and its ultimate closure.

The open door of the dreamer indicates that he is recep-
tive and that he indeed wishes to receive. By bringing his
mother into his bedroom, which is an extension of himself,
he is incorporating her into his life and his world. Revealing
the dreamer's desire for maternal affection and nurturing, his
mother's hand touches or runs over his forehead—or his
head from afar—in a way that makes contact palpable. Being
run over by a hand signifies that the hand has left an impression. The use of the word "ran" endows the mother's hand
with the motive ability of feet or wheels to carry one forth
into the distance.

In that the dreamer's mother was hospitalized for emotional reasons rather than physical problems, as she was an
otherwise healthy young woman, the dream may indeed
have predictive value based on the uncanny intuitive percep-
tiveness of the dreamer.

☽

The following are two more prophetic dreams, this time of the designer **Katarina**:

> *I saw my sister all the way up in the sky, and she was holding the hand of her daughter. Suddenly I see her fall all the way down to the ground, where she falls inside a very large hole with water. She disappears into the hole with her daughter. (The next day my brother-in-law telephoned me with the news that my sister had gone to the hospital, as she had suffered a nervous breakdown. Her daughter had to go with her, and had to remain there for a long while, as she needed to speak with the doctors and act as translator for her mother.)*

Seeing one's sister all the way up in the sky signifies an admixture of two assessments: The sister is both revered and viewed as having her head in the clouds, finding it hard to come down to earth. Her heightened angelic position changes, though, to its reverse as the sister literally "falls" from grace. The downward free-fall is symbolic of a mental collapse in that the sister disappears into the hole that she falls into. Disappearing into the water instead of emerging from the water represents a kind of death in that it is the symbolic opposite of birth. As the hole has water in it, the sister is submerged as though she is lost in her unconscious. As the sister cannot keep her head above water, she will sink. To be sure, this is not a scene of prosperity; this is a difficult time.

Katarina's dream had prophesied her sister's mental collapse down to the last detail. She had seen her sister's daughter disappearing into the hole along with her mother because the daughter's everyday existence changed too, as she had to stay with her mother at the hospital on a daily basis.

In Katarina's following prophetic dream, the effect is seen, but not the cause:

Six years ago I dreamt of my other sister from Rhodes. I saw the inside of her house and knew that something was wrong. Trouble, crying, pain. Then I saw my sister crying and screaming and waving her arms around as if she was in great pain. (A few days later my sister called me to tell me that she just found out that her husband, who had gone to Athens on business, had died of a heart attack.)

Within this double prophesy dream, Katarina not only knows that something is wrong in her sister's household before her sister does, but she also knows that a tragedy has occurred before the actual event (the death of her brother-in-law), which causes the sister to be crying with pain over the loss of her husband.

Seeing the inside of her sister's house—where the house represents the being—signifies Katarina's empathic nature. She intuits her sister's suffering, her pain, and her innermost emotions. Visually threadbare, with no disguised symbols or images, the dream relies on feeling and sensing rather than reason and underscores the dreamer's heightened sense perception, which may be a clue as to why she has prophetic ability.

F.C.D.L.T.'s dream of Friday, November 3, eerily predicted the assassination of Israel's president Yitzhak Rabin on Saturday, November 4, 1995. The dream is as follows:

I had an incredibly weird dream which I did not understand until the world events of Saturday. I dreamt that someone came up to me to tell me the King of Solomon was dead. I had no idea who he was. This news deeply upset me. I was crying and everyone around me was crying. (When I woke up I had tears running down my cheeks.) Suddenly I found myself in a drawing room set out like the one in our home in London, which had burnt down, killing my sister, three years before. I was sitting on the sofa with my shoes and feet up. I heard he had died in a fire. Then someone behind me sitting in a row of seats arranged for the eulogy said how badly mannered I was to put my feet on the sofa! How was I brought up? I went to sit on a chair and just kept crying. The people believed that I had been his mistress because I was crying so much! Then I saw him laid out as the great Egyptians were once they were dead. He had a long face with an E.T. (shaped) head, old, white hair, and he was thin. Somehow I knew that he was the author and inventor of the Barbar *books!*

The event that preceded the above dream is equally as strange as the dream's foreboding message. During an opening meditation in her monthly Reiki session, the dreamer had to leave the circle, as she was feeling faint. The feeling overwhelmed her precisely at the third position (solar plexus), which is involved with the survival instinct. After fainting, the dreamer awakened, feeling that she been somewhere "where [she] was shown or given some vitally important information," which may have been incorporated into her dream the following morning. The dreamer also made reference to someone from the session named Babs—she said, "Babs held my head, trying to get me back."

The dreamer's deceased sister, Barbara, was often called Babs, and the person from the Reiki session had another name entirely. The question remains, though, as to why the dreamer chose to give this individual the personal pseudonym Babs, as pseudonyms are used in the service of repression, to hide recognition from rising into consciousness. Curiously, the pseudonym chosen was an attempt of the unconscious to specifically unveil within the dreamer her immense feelings of survivor's guilt. Hence, the dreamer felt faint precisely at the third position, which involves survival, and mentions, "Babs held my head, trying to get me back."

As the dreamer found herself in a drawing room similar to her home in London that had burnt down, a partial meaning becomes clear: The dreamer's intent to find herself or gain recognition through the dream in the hopes that the dream will draw out unresolved emotional pain.

The dreamer's self-critical phrase, "How was I brought up?"—elicited from a voice coming from behind (representing the past and, more specifically, the deceased sister)—indicates that the dreamer was not raised well enough, and signifies despair over the fact that she herself did not die and was therefore not brought up in the way of her deceased sister. The dreamer's excessive crying over the man's death leads people to believe that she was his <u>mistress</u>. [The word "mistress" contains an anagram for the word "sister"]. As if we needed more proof of the personal meaning of the dream, the dead man is somehow mysteriously identified as the author of the "Barbar" books, underlined to bring attention to the purposeful misspelling of the actual title—Babar. Here, the unconscious is boldly revealing the sister's name, Barbara.

King Solomon, who meets his death through fire, is on one level the dreamer's sister, whose maiden name was Sanderman, and who died in a fire. Yet on a wholly different level he is the assassinated President Rabin of Israel, who meets his death through gunshot fire. Yet, in that the prophetic message contained within the dream was presented alongside the personal message of familiar symbolism, the interpretation was deflected away from the impersonal prophetic to the personal. Unfortunately, because of the dreamer's own painful associations and the action of repression, the dream was not understood until the assassination event became known to the world.

Upon viewing the faces of President Rabin and his temporary successor, Shimon Peres, the dreamer realized that the man she had seen laid out at the eulogy was a facial combination of both men. This prophesied that Shimon Peres would step down and would not succeed to the presidency.

Are these preceding dreams really prophetic, or are they just uncanny coincidences? Are they the midnight musings of intuitive minds, of dreamers who are more finely tuned to what is perceived as being the random static of the universe? You, the reader, must decide.

17

Prophetic Instruction
or Inspirational
Dreams

DREAMS THAT PREDICT CHARACTER

A dream that predicts character may be viewed as an in-
stigator of truth in that the character assessment presented within the dream is one that was initially made
during consciousness, but not reflected upon. The dream is
the vehicle that connects the dreamer with situational cues
that have been externally perceived prior to the dream. Regarding prophesy, however, these dreams are categorized as
after-the-fact, as the individual character in question often
reveals his true nature well before the dreamer remembers
his or her former dream.

It may be remembered that an example of a predictive
character dream (see Chapter 1, The Prophetic Dream) may
be found in the dream of the hapless businessman **Mr. L**,
who made an incorrect conscious assessment of his new employee Mr. K, a positive assessment that was contradicted by

the negative image Mr. K's character displayed in Mr. L's evening dream. Several years down the road, and after the loss of his business, Mr. L sadly recalled the extent to which his dream corroborated the sinister character and actions that Mr. K was later to reveal.

Another example of an undiagnosed dream predicting character was dreamt by **Jacques D'Arc**, the father of the innocent sixteen-year-old peasant girl, Jeanne D'Arc, who later was canonized as Saint Joan of Arc, before she marched off into battle leading France to victory. The father's dream is as follows:

I dreamt I saw my daughter with soldiers. She was walking off with them.

The fact that Jacques' unconscious mind would have made such an unusual pairing by connecting his daughter with soldiers should have revealed to him his daughter's innate sense of duty, her adventurous and courageous nature, and most of all her patriotic zeal. Whereas walking off signifies marching forward and is associated with religious or nationalistic fervor, leaving home represents the independent spirit of someone who exchanges personal intimacies and the conveniences of home for the impersonal glories of one's country. Yet Jacques misinterprets his predictive dream in the worst possible way, worrying over his daughter's loose morals.

Another dream that correctly predicted the character of a woman's husband was dreamt by **Lindsay**. Her dream follows:

> *My husband presents me with a huge bouquet of*
> *flowers. I unwrap the cellophane and untie the rib-*
> *bons. There are so many roses that they do not fit in the*
> *vase. I try to take out some of the roses, but I get*
> *pricked by a thorn I did not see. The vase is now*
> *wobbly, and I am afraid it will get knocked over and*
> *broken. My finger is bleeding, but my husband is*
> *still smiling. I show him my hand, and he says, "You*
> *see, I always think of you," as he walks away into an-*
> *other room and closes the door. He is in there with a*
> *businesswoman friend of his that I do not like (both in*
> *reality and in the dream). I hear them laughing inside*
> *the room. I put on a Band-Aid.*

Once again, this is a predictive dream specimen whose
presentation of character goes unnoticed until it is too late.
For hidden within the roses and the ribbons is the thorn of deception, which pricks the finger of the dreamer and symbolically draws blood from her heart.

A seemingly charming and romantic husband bestows
flowers upon his wife. In the wording of the dream he presents his wife with flowers; in other words, he gifts her in the
material sense. But in that the flowers have to be unwrapped
and the ribbons untied, there is plenty that needs looking
into. The cellophane wrapping signifies the transparency of
the situation, yet the dreamer is not perceptive. The act of not
paying attention proves painful, as the finger of the dreamer
is pricked by that which she does not see.

The vase symbolizes the dreamer in the precarious position of trust and belief—a receptacle in danger of being top-
pled over or broken by an excessive amount of roses or an
unctuous display of affection that proves false. When the
bleeding finger is shown to the husband, he is still smiling.

His caring words "I think of you" contradict his actions as he walks away into another room without a second thought. Worse, he closes the door on his wife's pain.

The wife, who shows him her hand, symbolizes her openness. There are no aces up her sleeve! In a situation that should invoke jealousy, the dreamer's reaction to hearing her husband laughing with a woman friend is most odd—the dreamer puts on a Band-Aid, in a symbolic representation of denial. She is covering her emotional wound. Even though the character of the husband is clearly delineated by his indifferent actions and his deceptive behavior, the dreamer is still in the dark. A year later, the husband leaves Lindsay for another woman. He walks out on her without even so much as a conversation, and certainly not a flower!

The following is a true account of a dream of **Calpurnia's** (as written by William Shakespeare in *Julius Caesar*) that predicts the character of Julius Caesar as he was perceived by his wife, and the collective character of the "lusty" Romans who will betray their emperor. Caesar had no idea that the Romans were plotting against him:

> *Calpurnia, here, my wife, stays me at home.*
> *She dreamt tonight: she saw my statue,*
> *Which like a fountain with an hundred spouts*
> *Did run pure blood; and many lusty Romans*
> *Came smiling, and did bathe their hands in it.*
> *And these days for warnings and portents*
> *And evils imminent; and on her knees*
> *Hath begg'd that I will stay at home today.*

The dream reveals how Calpurnia saw her husband—as a statue cold and immovable as stone. She sees his public stature rather than the private sentient being. Calpurnia's dream characterizes Caesar as unfeeling and unreasonable, as he is not affected by and does not listen to Calpurnia's begging. As though convinced of his greatness or invincibility, Caesar does not heed his wife's warning. He becomes humanized only through death, when he bleeds from his numerous stab wounds. Perhaps having a different character would have saved his life.

Skittish over Calpurnia's unheeded dream, Augustus Caesar, grand-nephew of Julius Caesar and heir to the throne, proclaimed a law that made all dreams about the Commonwealth the property of the Commonwealth in that the dreams had to be announced publicly in the marketplace.

The following dream of author **Jennifer Belle** predicts the character of a long relationship just before its breakup:

We are kissing each other through a cluster of plasticine bubbles. I can see his lips, but I am kissing the bubble.

The longing is for the passionate fullness of a physical relationship in which the lips become a symbolic synecdoche—the kissing part is overvalued as being representative of the whole person. Yet the communion of lips is not permitted, as there is no longer direct contact, particularly in the area of feelings.

The cluster of plasticine bubbles symbolizes protection from breakage; the fragile love relationship needs to be bubble wrapped. The bubble is what can burst; it signifies something insubstantial or ephemeral (the froth on the café latte)! The bubble is transparent, and Jennifer can see through the mythic romantic ideal just before it pops.

Yet the plasticine bubbles also represent the private constellations of another identity—the worlds within worlds of what we cannot know in someone else.

DREAMS THAT PREDICT LIFE DIRECTION

The philosopher Henry More asks this question: "The gods throw their lines as we throw ours for the fish, and they bait the lines with dreams, and how can we help but leap at them?" This means that dreams are inspirational in that they lead us on. Indeed, as we shall see, many dreams have been able to predict life direction, but only to the extent that these dreams were assiduously and willfully followed. But were these dreams predetermined externally and independent of the dreamer? This necessarily implies that the dream is presented *to* the dreamer from a source unknown—More's gods, perhaps—and not *from* the dreamer as the manifestation of an unconscious wish. Does the dream present foresight or hindsight?

One thing is certain: As the inspirational aspect of a predictive dream cannot be denied, the dream itself may be the catalyst that steers the dreamer in a certain direction; an internal or unconscious influence may be stronger than an external one. The following prophetic dream was dreamt by the fashion designer **Oleg Cassini:**

I have arrived by boat. Many people greet me with "I'm so glad you could come." I'm in Hollywood, surrounded by movie stars, recognizing faces from American movies, like Clark Gable. A beautiful darkhaired actress with light eyes and golden skin is in love with me. I'm a famous fashion designer.

It was Christmas of 1936, and Oleg Cassini was living in fascist Italy. War was imminent, and the way of life was disintegrating. Oleg's glamorous dream was definitely one of wish fulfillment, yet it was also a prophetic tool in that the future proved it true in every way. Indeed, the motivated Mr. Cassini followed his dream, journeying by steamer to the United States, where he became a fashion designer—as designer of choice to First Lady Jacqueline Bouvier Kennedy, perhaps the most famous and respected designer of the century, whose name has become a household word. He married the consummately beautiful movie star Gene Tierney.

However, what seems a prophetic dream is really Oleg coming to grips with an awareness of his own talents and his desire to fulfill them. The dream bolsters his self-confidence. In other words, the dreamer's self-knowledge inspires him with the drive to fulfill his wish consciously. By surrounding and immersing himself in another world, another setting, he has recognized all that he wants in life.

Arriving by boat reflects a wish to cross over to another world. The boat symbolizes the rite of passage. Being welcomed from the water represents a birth, a new life, a new start. Hearing people say "I'm so glad you could come" is the desire to be well-received and appreciated. Importantly, Oleg's arrival has been noted—"to have arrived" means that one has achieved success and recognition. But the dream wish is not just granted; the fame must be earned. Thus, by envisioning himself a fashion designer Oleg fashions the life he aspires to, as a designer symbolizes someone with a scheme, plan, or purpose.

New identity dreams usually represent admired figures whom the dreamer wishes to bond with in the hopes of experientially understanding the persona behind the history. The following dream of young **Jacqueline Bouvier** is oddly prophetic in that it was dreamt nearly a year before her auspicious meeting with John F. Kennedy:

> *(A fragment of a daydream/dream recollection as told to Jackie's stepbrother, Hugh D. Auchincloss III, in the summer of 1950:) We were in a castle, just after walking through the medieval walled town of Carcassonne in southern France, when I imagined myself a grand heroine like Joan of Arc.*

In reiteration of what has been stated many times previously, homes symbolically refer to the inner, walled-in private space that encloses the being and are considered reflections of the personality; therefore, the more palatial the home, the grander the sense of self. The castle, as an imposing domicile, represents the majestic wisdom of an old soul, the remoteness of a personality, and often reveals the wish for a protected and insulated existence. A castle symbolizes a sense of elevation and aloofness—raised above the mainstream of life—and denotes a certain inaccessibility.

The ancient setting of Carcassonne, a medieval walled town, may have been the antecedent that inspired Jacqueline with heroic thoughts of defending one's town against invaders. This suggests why Jackie imagined herself to be like Joan of Arc, who rose with inexorable strength above the mundane fears of mortality and vulnerability. Identifying with a martyr reveals Jackie's romantic nature, her imaginative flair for the dramatic, her adventurous spirit and innate sense of valor. It also reveals a profound gift of prophesy. In 1960, one short decade later, Jackie inhabited a symbolic castle, the White House (code termed "castle" in 1963 by the U.S. Secret Service Communications Agency) and became the ultimate martyr of the twentieth century. Interestingly, the daydream can also be interpreted as a prelude to the saintly Camelot era of her invention.

Suave actor **Peter Graves** had the following dream, which he did not deem prophetic until many years later, when he re-experienced the dream in a state of bewildered déja vu:

> *In my recurring childhood dream, I would find myself walking in a room that was fairly large but of indeterminate size, curious about where I was going. There were iron or metal bars from floor to ceiling, spaced out in odd ways. I would wander through them with a sense of familiarity and confidence. (Later, many years after my dream, I was on a sound stage of a motion picture set. I looked up and saw all of these metal stands— those floor-to-ceiling iron bars—that all the lights are put on, and it dawned on me: This was my dream!)*

In a room full of bars, a very young Mr. Phelps seems to be on an impossible mission of his own, the mission to adulthood, in that he finds himself. Finding oneself represents the foremost maturational wish: to discover who one really is and in which direction one's life is headed. The room that Peter walks through symbolizes his sense of self, which, although deemed fairly large, is of an indeterminate nature. In other words, Peter's dream is a manifestation of his desire to satisfy his curiosity about the future.

The bars signify something stable to hold on to, and although symbolic of the dreamer's rites of passage, the floor-to-ceiling iron or metal bars appear as markers of time rather than restrictive barriers, as they are widely spaced and allow

Peter the confidence to wander through and beyond. Yet, as the bars are sensed as familiar, they may represent something from the past: a jungle gym, perhaps, whose iron bars are meant to grasp hold of in order to ascend to a higher place, a higher level of personal growth or strength. In a paranormal sense, the familiar bars have already been seen in the future.

Within the dream, however, as opposed to climbing upward, the dreamer moves forward. Motion is continuous—and, in retrospect, the dream's prophetic essence—as the dreamer wanders through into his future. (Years later, Peter encounters the self-same bars, now realized as light stands, on a sound stage of a motion picture set.) The prophetic symbolism of the dream underscores Peter's intuitive nature.

The following prophetic dream was dreamt by actress and singer **Katharine Mehrling** many months before she came across a play about the life of Edith Piaf, her favorite singer, and nearly a year before she would star as Piaf in the musical *Piaf*, which would make its debut on the German stage:

> *I am sitting in an arena surrounded by a lot of people. Piaf was sitting in the middle, a little to the left. I sat a step below her. She put her hand on my head like a blessing. I felt happy.*

As Katharine is sitting in an arena surrounded by a lot of people, she seems to be in the middle (caught up with something); she is already positioned in a similar space of the room as her idol Piaf, who is also sitting in the middle. Katharine has incorporated Piaf into her space, as a room or an arena is a representative of the self or the being. Being seated to the left suggests that Piaf is in the dreamer's past. Being seated below Piaf allows the dreamer to gaze upward at Piaf in a heavenly direction, and also signifies the dreamer's modest respect—she is not yet ready to be on the same artistic level as her idol.

The many directions specified in the dream—left, middle, and below—represent the dreamer's need for direction or guidance, which she receives through the blessing from the deceased Piaf. Because the dreamer is seated lower than Piaf, her head is touched from above, in what is symbolically interpreted as a laying on of the hands, which is healing and restorative. Katharine is happy because within the dream a spiritual connection is made between herself and Piaf. Katharine sits at the right hand of her idol or god.

The dream is prophetic in that Katharine goes on to portray Piaf on the German stage, as though Piaf had visited the dreamer to inspire her on. Perhaps the nurturing pat on the head transferred some of Piaf's luminous and magical energy into Katharine's spirit as Katharine continues (as of this writing) to play Piaf to standing ovations.

The following recurring childhood prophetic dream was dreamt by the merchandising genius **Gale Hayman,** co-founder of the enormously successful Georgio Beverly Hills boutiques and fragrance:

I had a recurring dream, which started when I was eight years old and continued throughout childhood, that I owned a retail store. I saw myself in the shop, which had lots of shelves. I was climbing the ladder and putting things up on the shelves. I even had the key to the store, and it was all very real.

In that the dreamer sees herself within the dream, she is one step removed from herself—an objective spectator. The shop, with its many shelves, represents Gale as having many levels of inspiration, eager to stack every one of them with products.

Climbing the ladder literally signifies that the eight-year-old dreamer already had an agenda—the wish to succeed, to ascend, and to become upwardly mobile. The dreamer is reaching the heights and mentally storing things away for future use.

The symbol of the key has profound significance, particularly in its relation to a prophetic dream. The dreamer unconsciously knows how to open the door to unlock the future. Quite literally, it appears that the young dreamer already has a key or an understanding of what the future holds in store for her, which is why the dream is experienced as being very real. The recurrence of the dream underscores the dream's importance and necessity in the life of the dreamer. The dreamer holds the key to her dream and future success, as her dream *is* the key.

The following prophetic problem-solving dream was dreamt by **Warren Avis**, founder of Avis Rent A Car and CEO of Avis Enterprises:

I had just come from the bomb base. I had to get somewhere. There was no transportation. I dreamt there was a terrible need for ground transportation. That's how I started Avis.

When he was not flying as an Air Force combat officer, Mr. Avis could not get anywhere on land, as transportation was scarce. His dream, therefore, was based on external factors and on solving a real problem. But in order to come up with solutions, one must first be aware of what needs to be solved. Thus, there is the recognition, "I had to get somewhere," symbolizing the desire to get ahead in the world, to go forward, to progress; it also suggests drive. More importantly, the dream is looking forward, which is a good indicator of a prophetic or predictive dream. The dream is looking for answers. The phrase "I had to . . ." intensifies the sense of urgency and spirit of determination. Noticing an existing external need reflects a perceptive and empathic nature, the ability to look beyond oneself. Mr. Avis, having just come down from the clouds, is on solid ground, involved with realistic goals.

The need for ground transportation suggests there is much to be covered and not enough time, but the wheels of inspiration have already been set in motion. As ground transportation moves one from one place to another, there is also the wish for social interaction—to move about in society. Thus, the wish of the dream may be to connect people, to bring people closer to their aspirations.

The following recurring identity dream was dreamt by a brilliant young German research scientist, **Ariel**, when he was only seven years old. What is incredible about this dream is that it clearly shows or predicts the direction that the dreamer's life will take, which is proof that the dreamer was already aware of his life choice and his desire to help mankind. Moreover, the dream may be viewed as a prophetic and inspirational tool in that even in low moments of personal despair the recalled dream serves as a constant source of inspiration to the dreamer:

I see myself in the universe. There is no gravity, and I am floating around in a sort of liquid environment (like what I experience underwater when I am scuba-diving). There are flashes of light. There are huge bub-

bles, which I realize are cells. I am riding on one of the cells as though the cell is a chariot. There was a war going on between the good cells and the bad cells. I am on a good cell fighting a bad cell. There are different colors around me. At first, the colors are relatively dark, but then they change to lighter colors. Then, in bright light, I find something to destroy the bad cells. Now there is pure white light, and I know that I have succeeded.

Seeing oneself in the universe immediately presents a larger view, as this is beyond the material world. Not having to deal with gravity suggests that nothing can weigh down the aspirations of the dreamer. It reflects his independent thinking in that he is going against the grain; he will not be restricted by boundaries or rules.

The flashes of light symbolize inspirational thoughts and ideas of discovery. The bubbles, which visually appear encased in a membrane, are creatively realized as cells. Whereas the cells phonetically render the symbolization of being imprisoned, riding a cell as if it were a chariot reveals the mastery of the dreamer, external to the cell, giving directions with the reins in his hand.

The war that is going on between the good and bad cells is a reference to sickness and health—ease and dis-ease. The dreamer, in fighting off the bad cells, is clearly identifying himself as a doctor or research scientist who is working for the benefit of mankind. The dark colors suggest sickness or death, and the light colors suggest well-being and life; this is remarkably consistent with current New Age views that espouse the curative nature of white light. (Imaging or visualizing white light entering the body is believed to have a curative effect.)

In what may have been a premonitory vision, in bright light or in the brilliance of the mind, the dreamer makes a discovery: He finds something that destroys the bad cells. Thus, he has succeeded is serving mankind.

In another view, as the dreamer is German, the bad cells may symbolize germs or something within the dreamer that he wants to combat. The dream is a wish fulfillment to the extent that the dreamer was himself a sickly child and thus desirous of good health. Having the good cells win represents an optimistic view, a constructive reasoning that leads to the empowerment of the young and powerless dreamer. As the dreamer succeeds in his mission within the dream, he is self-empowered and inspired to pursue a career in molecular research. (The dreamer is concurrently working on finding out why the lens of the eye is the only part of the body that is not susceptible to cancer and studying marine biology for underwater clues as to the shark's cancer immunity.)

Although previously mentioned and interpreted (see Chapter 1, The Prophetic Dream), the following prophetic dream of young fashion designer **Katarina** is noted once again in its entirety, as the dream predicts her life direction. What is more romantically prescient than dreaming of one's future spouse, down to his facial appearance and coloring, particularly when the dreamer is already engaged to another man? The dreamer was living in Greece, about to be married to a blond, blue-eyed man, when her dream envisioned a dark-haired, dark-eyed man standing in front of the New York City skyline. It was a dream that started the dreamer thinking. It was a dream that changed her life.

A tall man in a black suit comes in front of me. He puts his arm around my waist and holds me. From where I am standing I see the whole New York City skyline. I recognize the Empire State Building, and in the distance the Statue of Liberty. The man says, "You are mine. You must marry me."

Months after this dream the young dressmaker arrived in America and found herself in New York City, standing in the precise location that the dream depicted. She then made the acquaintance of a tall stranger in a black suit, who was quite taken with her. According to the dreamer, the stranger's face was an exact double of the face of the man within her dream. They married shortly after this meeting.

Of course, it could be argued that the dream was merely a manifestation of a wish fulfilled by the willful determination of a young dreamer eager to move to New York City, and that the dream divulged the dreamer's dissatisfaction with her present fiancé and her need for liberation (she recognizes the Statue of Liberty). Yet the dream remains an uncanny event in that the face of the strange man pictured within the dream is the actual face of the man that the dreamer marries. Once again, however, the cause of such an occurrence may be chalked up to the determination of the dreamer to seek out the man of her dreams. In other words, this man must conform to what she construes as a desirable type of male.

The following dream was dreamt by the invincible **Ivana Trump** after her very public divorce from "the Donald." The dream has a predictive element as it reveals the positive direction her post-divorced life will take:

I had a dream that I was competing in the winter Olympics and had hit the slopes at 100 miles an hour, leaving the rest of the skiers, many of whom I had

known from the Czech team, far behind. I was com-
pletely alone on the slopes and felt free as a bird,
soaring through the air without a care in the world
and, of course, knowing that I had won the gold medal.
When I reached the finish line the only spectators there
were my three children. They were clapping and shout-
ing, "Mom, you're a winner! Mom, you're a winner!
Mom, you're a winner!" I was suddenly awakened
by my three young children and two dogs who had
run into my bedroom at some unearthly hour in the
morning and were jumping on my bed. To me this was
better than any gold medal!

Whereas emotions usually sink to the lows of the valleys after a divorce, Ivana's optimistic unconscious positions itself on the peak. Initially, dreaming of being atop a mountain may be viewed as the result of hard and arduous work and symbolizes a measure of achievement. Yet, this position of prominence is difficult to maintain—on the steep "slopes" of life Ivana must watch out for the pitfalls—the ruts or moguls (especially *moguls*) along the way that may trip her up and bring her down! Leaving the rest of the skiers "far behind" reveals Ivana's independent spirit and sense of self worth— she is as comfortable breaking away from the crowds as from a highly publicized marriage. Not only can she make it on her own, she is a trendsetter as she leaves tracks behind for others to follow.

Hitting the slopes at "100 miles an hour" signifies passionate determination—the fast pace underscores Trump's drive and ambition. In terms of personal fulfillment, Ivana's unconscious is already aware that she is a winner in the *long run*, as the "gold medal" that is won is the *mother* of all medals.

The real prize is not lost sight of—her wonderful children are by her side, cheering her on.

DREAMS THAT PREDICT THE OUTCOME OF A RELATIONSHIP

What was formerly interpreted as a wish-fulfillment dream in another one of my books is re-presented here as a dream that is also inherently predictive in nature. The dream is interesting not only because it contains classic divorce imagery but in that it prefigures a divorce. To this extent, the dream successfully predicts the outcome of a marital relationship. It was dreamt by **Edith Rockefeller**, a daughter of John D. Rockefeller, Sr., while she was separated, geographically rather than legally, from her husband and the tensions of her marriage during a two-year self-imposed exile in Switzerland. She had mentioned the dream to Carl Jung before embarking on a long analysis with the noted psychoanalyst. During the time of her analysis, Edith was once again separated from her husband and the numerous problems within her marital relationship. This time the separation would widen into an unbridgeable gulf between them that would result in a swift divorce.

Edith had told Jung she dreamt of a tree that had been struck by lightning and split in two. Whereas Jung had thought her dream a symptom of latent schizophrenia, the dream was actually revealing in no uncertain terms her desire to split from—to sever ties with—her husband, which is verifiable by her eventual divorce several years later. The lightning either symbolizes an electrifying idea—a powerful bolt from the blue (the unconscious)—or the wish for divine intervention. The bohemian Edith was literally struck by lightning at the force and ferocity of her unrepressed wish to divorce—to split something traditionally solid and rooted. The tree, as both a representation of the male phallus (the trunk) and the female genitalia (the leafy area), is a symbol of the marital union that must be rendered asunder, as this is a viable way to separate the male from the female, the husband from wife.

Picturing the dream of the split tree is a way of making divorce possible. The task is so frightening a prospect and one so difficult to achieve that divine intervention is needed. The wish of the dream is that the marital union be severed, no matter what the ramifications. And what better external attribution is there? The fulfilled wish is that the split occurs as a result of nature's tempestuous whim and not Edith's emotional inability to cope with the tedious responsibilities and fidelities of the marriage bond.

The following intuitive or prophetic anxiety dream preceded the breakup of a Manhattan designer's marital relationship. **Katarina's** dream thematically reveals jealousy and anguish over her spouse's possible infidelity and amazingly intuits her husband's romantic involvement with another woman. The dream is as follows:

Looking into the room of my bedroom I suddenly saw my husband. I saw a big white mink coat sprawled across the bed. I saw another woman prepared to go someplace with my husband. I heard her say, "We have to leave." I could not hear where they were going. Then I was awakened from sleep by the sound of the front door slamming closed. I walked around the apartment and realized that my husband had just left. I rushed to the window and saw my husband with a big suitcase going into a white limousine waiting on the street. He had left for Las Vegas with a strange woman, without telling me.

What is fascinating about this dream is its intuitive nature. The dreamer has somehow sensed the departure of her husband simultaneously with his actual leaving, for he leaves both in the dream and in reality. It could be argued, however, that the sound of the door slamming is what causes the dreamer to rapidly link the sound of departure with her unfaithful husband, who has already some time before metaphorically exited from the conjugal bedroom of trust and fidelity.

In that a room in a house symbolizes the person, the idea of another woman must have previously entered Katarina's conscious mind as surely as another woman has entered her bedroom within the visualization of the dream. More specifically, the bedroom represents the marital union. Being outside the bedroom suggests that the dreamer is beyond the conjugal realm—on the outside looking in. Seeing and overhearing an event wherein things are happening without her consent reveals that Katarina is in a powerless position. Outside of the marital loop Katarina is at best a bystander to conjugal perquisites.

The big white mink coat is symbolically perceived as a luxury item, which appears in actuality sprawled along the street transfigured into a waiting white limousine. Clearly, the fear of spousal departure from the home was already in Katarina's unconscious, but it took a dream to convince Katarina to put an end to her denial. Suddenly she sees her husband as he really is, and she is prepared for what is to follow. As the dream states, the other woman *is* prepared, whereas Katarina is somehow at a loss.

The many signals of marital dissolution and spousal unfaithfulness that seem to have been repressed during the dreamer's wakefulness have found their avid audience in the unconscious realm of the dreamworld.

The following dream is an example of negative self-affirmation, wherein a personal affirmation is achieved at the expense, detriment, demoralization, or minimization of another individual. This is the dream of an ex-husband of a former patient, who had relayed his dream to my patient while he was still her fiancé. The day before the dream, my patient had asked her fiancé to assist her in moving from her apartment. He had helped her load up shopping carts with objects from her home. This was the daytime residue of the dream that the ex-husband hastened to tell my patient, as he claimed that this dream of his was what convinced him of his love for her. His dream is as follows:

You were in a shopping cart, and you were blind, and I was pushing you around.

The symbol of the shopping cart is two-fold: It suggests a constrictive cage and at the same time objectifies the fiancée into an item pulled from a shelf. Being blind further diminishes the autonomy of the fiancée, who is viewed as being helpless, dependent, and in need of guidance and direction. She cannot see and therefore has no foresight into the situation (the cramped space) she has gotten herself into.

The wheels of the cart indicate the immobility of her legs—her entrapment. The dreamer (the husband to be) is the one in control, the one who is doing the steering, the one who is pushing her around, which seems to be the dreamer's actual wish—to push his fiancée around. The dream self-empowers the dreamer at the expense of someone else's ability to fend for themselves.

In reality, time would prove the dreamer (the husband) an extremely controlling and manipulative individual, one who became both verbally and physically abusive. Had my patient interpreted her fiancé's dream correctly, she would never have married him and would have avoided the difficult and painful experience of a divorce.

DREAMS THAT PREDICT THE OUTCOME OF AN EVENT OR DISCOVERY

Dreams that make discoveries are predictive in nature, as they foresee an outcome. The chemist Dmitry Mendeleyev, who was attempting to develop a system to classify the chemical elements according to their atomic weights, which would enable him to predict the discovery of some unknown elements, claims to have dreamt of such a system—what we now call the periodic table.

Descartes supposedly realized that science and philosophy should be linked after a dream he had in which he discovered a dictionary that he read and also an anthology of poetry. He interpreted the dream to mean that observational scientific reasoning should be applied to philosophic inquiries.

Elias Howe, by discovering within his dream the correct placement of where to put the hole at the end of the sewing needle, was able to finalize and make operational his invention of the sewing machine. His predictive dream follows:

> *I was captured by a tribe of savages. The king roared, "Elias Howe, I command you on pain of death to finish this machine at once." The tribal lord ordered his warriors to execute me. Then I noticed that at the pointed end of each warrior's spear was an eye-shaped hole.*

The tribe of savages symbolizes the metaphorical uninhibited inhabitants of the id, who fulfill their every instinct and drive, for the land of the id is where the creative and inspirational energies never sleep. This part of the dream is meant to spur Elias on to thoughts of great clarity and significance. The king represents the father figure, the paternal reprimand and demand all in one. The threat of being executed is actually a wish fulfillment that contains the fervent desire to be able to execute a workable needle for his machine. The end of each spear could be interpreted as meaning that Elias Howe was literally at the end of his tether. The spear is the spearhead idea and the male phallus—the driving force in an action or an endeavor. The eye-shaped hole represents vision or sight. The hole at the end of the spear is the orifice of the phallus from which the seeds of life spill forth—this is the wish for creative inspiration. Thus, the wish of the dream is to bring to fruition Howe's invention or creation.

Coincidentally, this wish was symbolized by the exact image that Elias Howe needed to see. More than anything else, the dream reveals how the unconscious mind works while we are sleeping, how involved it remains in the solving of our daily problems.

Dreams that contain religious symbolism, such as icons or visitations of Jesus or the Virgin Mary, often occur during lows in life situations. In addition to being spiritually inspirational, these dreams often foster thoughts beyond the mundane world of the material, which often prepare the dreamer for some terrible hardship that is yet to occur. This is the predictive element. The following religious dream was dreamt by **Helen Sanders**, a radio show producer, while she was between jobs:

I was back in the home I grew up in (in reality, the house had burned to the ground years before). In the living room, next to the upright piano I had played and practiced on in youth, in the corner, was a statuette-sized Mother Mary. She threw spheres rotating in midair to my two brothers and me. I received two. One I understood was for my mother, whom I have taken care of and looked after most of my life because of a mental breakdown. The other sphere was for me. My brothers did not walk but floated ahead of me on their journey with their spheres. I felt I was being led through my journey by the spirit of Mary, but that part of my burden would be carrying the sphere (the ball) for my mother. I was being shown that everything in my physical world was not solid as it appeared to be—and that it was a substance that barely existed, a substance that was penetrable. For some reason, though, when I reached the kitchen area, there was a lead surface that I could not pierce through. I did not know why at the time of the dream.

Months after this dream Helen lost two rooms of storage that included her piano and other treasured possessions—furniture handmade by her father and numerous irreplaceable childhood photographs. Although devastated by her loss, Helen managed to recollect her strange and mystical dream, which she interpreted as being a forewarning about how to deal with the fire that was to come. She viewed the dream as a lesson about the meaning of life and the necessity of letting go of material things, as they were shown to be transitory or immaterial, but definitely not solid.

The statuette of Mother Mary symbolizes the wish to be nurtured and cared for. The statuette that threw rotating spheres or balls to the dreamer symbolically reveals that the weight of the world is in the dreamer's hands, as the dreamer is the one who is responsible for her mother. In a paranormal sense (in that seraphim have been described as being able to rotate themselves into spheres or discs), the angels are leading the dreamer on a journey toward a specific wisdom. The rotation of the spheres symbolizes the circularity of time, which signifies that life is not without its highs and lows; in other words, what comes around goes around. The subliminal message behind the rotation of the spheres is meant to enlighten the dreamer, which is why she floats. The knowledge that nothing is solid will be useful later on when the dreamer loses many possessions in a fire.

In no uncertain terms, this was a period of instability for the dreamer, which is transfigured by the physical world of the dream appearing as a nonsolid, nonpermanent, non-stable substance. This may symbolize the mental state of the dreamer's mother, as the mother had had four mental break-downs. As the house represents who we are, going through the house represents an effort to come to terms with and understand one's persona. The lead surface in the kitchen area that the dreamer could not pierce through represents the mind, in that the kitchen is the place where one eats with one's mouth and thus represents the uppermost region of the body. This suggests that at the time of the dream the dreamer was trying to penetrate the dream's meaning, but was unable to do so.

☽

The writer **Isabel Allende** writes about her predictive-outcome "prophetic pregnancy" dreams, saying, "I knew when I was pregnant with my two children before there was any sign. And I knew what the sex of the children would be. I always see the boy or the girl in the dream." She also claims to have been able to predict the sex of her grandchildren. The predictive outcome dream also included the name of the child. Allende writes: "I never had to think of a name because [the children] already had names in the dream. Names that I would never have chosen because nobody in my family had those names." Allende claims that her dreams are never wrong simply because her dream "knows."

In or around 1976, novelist and poet **Reynolds Price** had a strange dream that he turned into a poem called "The Dream of a House," from his book *Vital Provisions*. Looking back, he realized that the dream had miraculously perceived that he had cancer nearly eight years before the doctors discovered it and many years before he had conscious symptoms. In 1984, Reynolds Price was diagnosed with cancer of the upper spine. The surgery and radiation that ensued left him paralyzed from the waist down. His predictive-outcome or discovery dream is as follows:

I'm this mysterious, solitary person, and there is some kind of guide beside me. I'm being led through this incredibly beautiful house by a man who keeps saying, "Well, this is yours, this beautiful place, and in it are all the pictures you've ever wanted, all the books. It's all here, you've got this." Then I say to the guide, "Well, this is fantastic. Am I going to be alone here?" And he says, "Oh no. Come with me," and he opens

*this closet in the front hall. It's a normal closet with
nice new clothes in it and hats. Then he pulls the
clothes aside, and there's this human being who's literally been crucified in the closet—this man who's obvi-
ously terribly beaten and mutilated, and he's hanging
on a cross. The guide just says, "This is yours forever.
This will be yours forever." (At the end of the dream, I
felt very happy. I woke up and thought, My God! What
kind of weird religious fantasy is this?)*

Both the mysterious solitary person and the guide are the
same being, that of the dreamer, as they are both in the same
room. Yet the guide is the initiator of wisdom, the Jungian
animus in the male psyche. As a house symbolizes the person, a beautiful house signifies that Reynolds Price has
a wonderful sense of his own persona. He views himself as a
self-contained and self-sufficient, fulfilled individual, in
that he has everything he wants and needs within him and
within his personal space. The pictures are the memories he
has stored over the years; the books are the information
he has acquired.

The dream is revelatory as a closet is opened and something hidden is exposed. The front hall closet represents the
frontal region of the brain. How fitting that this frontal area
governs planning and consciousness, for the dreamer will
have to prepare for major life changes. As Reynolds is to take
on a new existence, new or different clothing must be worn,
which is why the items in his closet are recognized as being
new. This indicates a change of heart or action—a new beginning. The dreamer's sense of self will be altered. Indicating that appearances are more than skin deep, the clothing
is pulled aside and a human being is discovered who has

been crucified. This is the sweeping aside of the material world of clothing for that of the spiritual world of the soul. The guide suggests that this being is the dreamer's own cross to bear. He says, "This is yours forever."

The predictive element within the dream is of symbolic form. The man nailed to the cross signifies total immobility, an immobility that Reynolds will experience as a result of spinal surgery that will leave him paralyzed from the waist down. The condition is unalterable and objectified as something that will remain forever with Reynolds.

What is particularly strange is the dreamer's reaction of happiness to his morbid finding of a mutilated and crucified man. Thus, the dream makes a predictive discovery: Reynolds gains the knowledge of personal suffering and a spiritual sense that will pull him through. Even when confronted with great hardship, he will find peace with himself.

Before writer **Anne Rice's** daughter was diagnosed with acute granulocytic leukemia, Anne had the following predictive-outcome dream:

> *I remember [my daughter] was very sick in the dream, and she was withering. She was turning blue and withering, and she had a blood disease.*

One cannot help wondering if Anne Rice's novelistic interest in vampires was triggered by her daughter's onset of leukemia, a disease of the blood, as her vampire series begins after the death of her child (see the section below, Writers' Nightmares: Dreams That Inspirationally Predict Novels). It is almost as if the dream envisions through literary eyes and is thus enabled to see through the daughter's skin and into her veins to diagnose or give a synopsis of the deficiency of white blood cells. Perhaps the blood has been depleted or sucked out by the thirsty fangs of an undead zombie.

Anne's dream exemplifies how mothers seem to have wired-in, uncanny, intuitive feelings about their offspring. Anne may have consciously picked up anxiety-provoking cues that she then defensively repressed into unconsciousness. As no mother wants to learn that her child is dying or seriously ill, the predictive dream is a manifestation of a mother's worst fears.

The following predictive dream was dreamt by the founder of *Quest* magazine, **Heather Cohane:**

> I have two pet tortoises. I dreamt that one of them was upside down and on top of the other tortoise. He was not moving, and I thought this odd. Upon awakening, I walked past the basin to check on the tortoises, and one tortoise was belly up atop the other—he had gotten his leg stuck and could not move. Had I not have helped him he would have died.

This is a dream that actually saw an event that had happened, or perhaps was happening at that precise moment, as in a photograph. The image of the tortoise not being right side up actually symbolized that something was very wrong. Fortunately, the dreamer believed enough in her dream to check on her tortoise. One might say this is what her dream *tortoise*!

The following predictive dream of **Richard Jenrette**, retired chairman of Donaldson, Lufkin and Jenrette and former chairman of Equitable, reveals the outcome in terms of his future lifestyle:

When I was in school I often had a recurring dream of being in a big house with white columns in front of it.

Growing up in North Carolina and having seen *Gone with the Wind* may have precipitated Mr. Jenrette's love of big houses with white columns. Yet from the perspective of the dream world, a home represents the human form and its basic characteristics, as it refers to the walled-in private space that encloses the being. In other words, the home is considered a reflection of the personality. Thus, the more palatial the home, the grander the sense of self.

Dreams involving architectural symbolism, such as columns or pillars, reveal the importance of having structure and order in one's life, of building or creating. Columns may also represent legs and thus, the wish to stand tall. As examples of classic Greek idealism, there is an emphasis on upholding ideas or ideals, for columns represent loftiness and the wish to be elevated to great heights. As columns are vertical supports that carry the weight of responsibility and literally hold up the roof, they are associated with strength and indicate Mr. Jenrette's supportive nature. The big house with white columns may symbolize the White House—the wish to be a leader. Thus, as chairman of his company, it seems that Mr. Jenrette was the architect of his own dream or that his dream was the prophetic architect of his life.

The real prophetic element of the dream is that Mr. Jenrette now owns five big houses with columns!

WRITERS' NIGHTMARES: DREAMS THAT
INSPIRATIONALLY PREDICT NOVELS

> *Tis we, who lost in stormy visions, keep*
> *With phantoms an unprofitable strife,*
> *And in mad trance, strike with our spirit's knife*
> *Invulnerable nothings.*
>
> PERCY BYSSHE SHELLEY

There are several notable instances in literature in which an author has dreamt of the existence of a character or story that was then brought to life on paper in novelistic form. These dreams are considered prophetic in that they result from divine inspiration or are predictive of a story that the dreamer will write in the future—a story known inwardly before it exteriorizes. In other words, the story that is given materializes some time later, in manuscript form at the bookstore!

Where divine inspiration is involved, the spiritual agent or muse acts as a vehicle bringing a message or story that in turn inspires the writer to create a work of fiction. In this situation, the writer falls asleep in an uninspired *tabula rasa* state of writer's block and awakens with a fully developed scenario. Similarly, when a suggestive thought is received during wakefulness, it is worked over and fully developed during the unconsciousness of sleep. As we shall see, predictive literary dreams often foretell an actual situation, an event that will happen to the writer in the future. The knowledge received within the dream may reveal the entire event or only a hint of what is to occur, and the writer must tap into his unconscious for more details. These dreams may also disclose an existing but unknown or disregarded somatic condition of the dreamer or of those around him.

Mary Godwin Shelley: The Monster Awakens

A fine example of a prophetic nightmare that gave way to an archetypal horror story is that of Mary Godwin Shelley's gothic masterpiece—indeed, *monsterpiece—Frankenstein.* Mary's nightmare prophesied the novel she would eventually write, as well as a series of extraordinary circumstances in her personal life. The antecedent that initiated Mary Shelley's prophetic and predictive dream is exquisitely gothic in overtone, as it set the scene for what was to follow.

At his villa in Geneva, Lord Byron and a group of friends, including Mary Godwin and her then-paramour Percy Bysshe Shelley, were reading aloud from a collection of German ghost stories. Inspired by hearing these tales of terror, Byron suggested to each of his guests that they write a horror story. Perhaps it was Mary's desire to fulfill Byron's unusual suggestion that resulted in her having a prophetic nightmare that very evening. In *Shelley the Purist*, Richard Holmes recounts Mary's dream:

> *My imagination, unbidden, possessed and guided me, gifting the successive images that arose in my mind with a vividness far beyond the usual bonds of reveries. . . . I saw the pale student of unhallowed arts kneeling beside the thing he had put together. I saw the hideous phantasm of a man stretched out, and then, on the working of some powerful engine, show signs of life, and stir with an uneasy, half-vital motion. Frightful must it be; for supremely frightful would be the effect of any human endeavor to mock the stupendous mechanism of the Creator of the world. . . . He sleeps, but he is awakened; he opens his eyes; behold, the horrid thing stands at his bedside, opening his*

> *curtain and looking on him with yellow, watery, but*
> *speculative eyes. . . .*

Upon fearfully awakening, Mary returned to the comforts of reality with the powerful realization that the creature in her dream, who had made her shudder from fright, would equally terrify others. Thus, she wrote out the nightmare's plot. According to Holmes, within the fifth chapter of *Frankenstein*, the pivotal chapter that describes Dr. Franken-stein's attempt to arouse the monster from his sleep, is the self-same scene visualized in Mary's nightmare.

But the questions remain: Upon whom did Mary model the pale student of unhallowed arts who kneels, god-like, "beside the thing that he had put together"? Upon what did Mary conceptualize the hideous monster? What could have inflamed her imagination during a dream state that was not already simmering during her waking hours?

It is reasonable to surmise that Lord Byron's proposal to create a horror story provided the stimulus Mary needed to tap into the collective unconscious during her dream state. Yet the plot of her story, her prophetic nightmare, may be viewed as an evolutionary remnant of the universal mind trying to come to terms with the mystery of creation, and with man's inherent fear of monstrous beings or creatures. As Mary tapped into the creative energy around her, it is al-most as if the scene that she dreamt had already existed. Mary just reined it in.

Although the scene within Mary's dream becomes the novel, the novel conversely becomes the conscious night-mare in that *Frankenstein* reveals deep psychological truths reflective of Mary's own tormented life. Foremost is her prophetic envisioning of the character of Dr. Victor Frankenstein, for he is a symbolic representation of her husband, Percy Shelley.

Percy Shelley was viewed as a pleasure seeking, self-involved cad. After leaving his wife and two children untended for, he ran off with sixteen-year-old Mary and her stepsister Claire in the hopes of a future *ménage à trois*. After Mary lost Shelley's baby during premature childbirth, her devastation was made greater by Percy's indifference to the child's death. (Several years later Mary lost another child due to Shelley's negligent and irresponsible nature. He demanded that Mary travel a great distance to meet him with their weak and fevered child.)

At the time of the nightmare, Mary had already lost one child and was pregnant with another, which must have factored heavily into her dream and eventual writing of *Frankenstein*. Anguishing over the loss of her child and feeling incompetent as a mother, Mary dreamt of an anomalous birth of a creature, for on some level she may have viewed herself as an unhallowed creator. Yet the dramatic scene of the birth within the dream, in which Victor brings a corpse back to life, functions as a wish fulfillment; it represents Mary's desire to bring her own child back from the dead.

More importantly, however, the dream reveals to what extent Mary felt usurped in her womanly function, fearing that she would not bear Shelley normal, healthy children. In an expression of her sense of self being nullified by the narcissistic Shelley and her own deep-rooted feelings of inferiority, Mary dreamt of a man, Dr. Frankenstein, who creates life without a woman. At this point in time, with her childbearing ability in doubt, Mary may have felt her presence in Shelley's world a gratuitous and superfluous one.

From another perspective, it is just as easy to view Mary's

prophetic dream as a story of a woman abandoned by her creator; her identification would lie with the creature, as if the entity of Percy Shelley's betrayal took on the body of the creature. If we look at Victor Frankenstein as the real creature, as the monster who irresponsibly creates life, it is easy to draw a parallel with the enormously insensitive Percy Shelley, whose arrogance and narcissism begot a philosophy that held no regard for people or their needs. In *Intellectuals*, Paul Johnson writes, "Shelley believed that society was totally rotten and should be transformed, and that enlightened man had the moral right and duty to reconstruct it." Like Dr. Frankenstein, Shelley is the ignoble "pale student" of creation with the self-endowed right to piece together humanity to suit himself and thus accommodate his own selfish desires.

In the dream, the doctor symbolizes Shelley's role of master presiding over Mary's role of his creature. In a Pygmalion sense, Percy Shelley cultivated Mary's talents. Mary was reconstructed or re-created by Shelley, as she was his intellectual and social inferior—an unformed being. Replicating the novel, Shelley grew increasingly dissatisfied with his creation (Mary) and started focusing on her stepsister, Claire, just as Dr. Frankenstein gave life to a creature that he would ultimately abandon.

It is the mystical nature of Mary's dream that provides the most chilling scenario, for within the fabric of the dream is a predictive element so uncanny that it cannot be disregarded— the dream foretells the actual manner in which Percy Bysshe Shelley will die.

Whereas Mary's novel prophetically concludes with the drowning of Dr. Frankenstein, who plunges off a boat into the freezing waters of the Arctic, the cold-hearted Shelley drowns in 1822 (four years after the completion of her novel) in a boating accident on the Mediterranean during a storm.

This prophesy, eerily foretold in her novel-from-a-dream, is an echo of Mary's unspoken yet virulent resentment of Shelley, which resembles the creature's growing resentment of his master. Another preternatural element predicts Mary's situation following Shelley's death. After Shelley drowns, Mary is left penniless, forced to leave the warmth of the continent for the cold of England, where she is shunned by society for her behavior. The creature, alone and abandoned, wanders over the frozen north.

Robert Louis Stevenson: Phantasmagoria and the Divided Self

British literature boasts yet another dream-induced tale of horror, Robert Louis Stevenson's *The Strange Case of Dr. Jekyll and Mr. Hyde*. For, as we shall see, what began as a terrifying nightmare ended as a prophetic dream that not only predicted the plot of a dark tale of dual personalities but remarkably foresaw what was then unrecognized: the clinical condition of bipolar disorder, commonly known today as manic-depression, along with the chemical method of treatment!

Whereas in early childhood Stevenson feared sleep, as it brought him frequent nightmares, in later years he became extremely dependent on those very dreams for his literary inspiration. (Stevenson's ideation for Jekyll and Hyde was dreamt during a time when he was suffering from writer's block.) Stevenson believed he had nocturnal visitations of "little people" or "brownies," whom he viewed as divine messengers, as they helped him bring ideas to fruition in the form of literature. More than likely, whatever was suppressed from consciousness actively manifested itself within his unconscious in the form of horrid visions attributed to the "brownies."

In *Robert Louis Stevenson*, Frank McLynn makes note of Stevenson's prophetic nightmare:

> *I had long been trying to write a story on this subject, to find a body, a vehicle, for that strong sense of man's double being which must at times, come in upon and overwhelm the mind of every thinking creature. For two days I went about racking my brains for a plot of any sort; and on the second night I dreamed the scene at the window, and a scene afterward split in two, in which Hyde, pursued for some crime, took the powder and underwent the change in the presence of his pursuers.*

In that it is known that Stevenson suffered from a series of emotional breakdowns, this dark aspect of Stevenson's personality was at the root of his prophetic nightmare. It is precisely at the point of the dream when Stevenson sees Mr. Hyde drink a mysterious potion, a chemical that turns Hyde into Jekyll, that his unconscious is zeroing in on a future remedy for Stevenson's own illness. His incredible dream envisions the use of antidepressive medication by indicating to Stevenson that ingesting a drug will alter or modify personality or one's chemical balance. Within the dream, the scene (phonetically rendered as "seen") that splits in two indicates the duality of Stevenson's perception.

Another reason Stevenson's nightmare is essentially predictive is that it demonstrates to him that there is an inherent split in his personality. What may not be consciously recognized is discerned within Stevenson's dream through the characters of Jekyll and Hyde in that they actualize his disorder. In naming his character Hyde, Stevenson reveals that he was intuitively aware of a hidden, unconscious part of his personality. Thus, his unconscious predicted how this dark side needed to be subdued.

Anne Rice: Bloodlines

As the death of a child is a mother's worst nightmare, here is a dream of Anne Rice that prophesies the death of her daughter and leads to the writing of her novel *Interview with a Vampire*. As we will see, Anne's prophetic dream, in which her daughter is viewed as dying of a blood disease, also predicts her ultimate obsession with blood and related vampire mythology. (Rice explores man's darker nature in her work, most notably in the *Vampire Chronicles*, which focus on the exploits of the sensuous and compulsive Vampire Lestat.)

Before Anne's daughter was diagnosed as having acute granulocytic leukemia, Anne dreamt the following disturbing nightmare:

> *[My daughter] was very sick in the dream, and she was withering. She was turning blue and withering, and she had a blood disease.*

Her dream eerily prefigured her daughter's future symptoms of turning blue and withering and unfortunately predicted her young daughter's death in 1972. In a manner of speaking, in that Rice's daughter died from a draining of the blood, a strong symbol presents itself, that of a vampire victim. Several weeks after her daughter's death, Anne Rice began vigorously writing her novel; she finished *Interview with a Vampire* in 1973. Because of the specificity of the subject matter, Rice's nightmare was doubly prophetic; it predicted her daughter's death from leukemia, a disease in which the blood is tainted with too many white blood cells, and her novel *Interview with a Vampire*, in which the vampire taints the blood of others, sucking them dry and killing them.

In an art-imitates-life scenario within the novel, the protagonist's victim, a beautiful young child named Claudia, is turned into a vampire and later adopted by the fanged protagonist, Lestat. The child tells Lestat that she is not his daughter, to which he answers, "Your mama's left you with us. . . . She knows we can make you very happy." The child responds, "I'm my mama's daughter," to which Lestat emphatically answers, "Not anymore." This is the voice of resignation of Anne Rice—the mother who has given over her child, her creation—to the world of literature, where she will remain immortalized. Yet, in that vampires are often referred to as zombies or the undead, Rice wishes for the eternal life of her daughter.

Rice's dream about her daughter also predicts the future character and tragic fate of Claudia within the novel. Claudia appears in later books in Rice's *Vampire Chronicles*, and reveals the writer's desire to preserve the spirit of her beautiful child through the creative act of writing. On another level, Rice's dream reveals her novelistic interest in getting beneath the surface to fix what is not flowing, the life blood of creation. Her dream image of withering may symbolize writer's block, that Rice was dried up, so to speak.

18

Prophetic Dreams That Predict Through Visitations of the Deceased

P rophetic dream visitations are exactly like those predictive dreams that foretell death, the outcome of events, the outcome of relationships, and life direction, with the exception that the prophetic message within these dreams is coming to the dreamer via the recognizable deceased. These dreams of visitation are often taken more seriously, as they come from a known source—a source that is seen to possess heightened knowledge. A dream that accurately predicts a future event in an expedient manner is so startling that the dream itself seems to go beyond any psychoanalytic interpretation and defy even the laws of scientific reasoning. Indeed, many of these predictive or prophetic dreams must be accepted as uncanny, particularly those in which the dreamer is given information regarding someone's approaching death. Still, there are those who will try to cite perfectly logical antecedents in the dreamer's realm of consciousness as causing the foreknowledge that comes to pass.

DREAMS THAT PREDICT OUTCOME OR
ARE INSTRUCTIONAL

The following is an instructional visitation dream that predicts outcome. The dreamer's deceased grandfather and step-grandmother are able to reassure the dreamer that the anxiety she is feeling prior to the dream is unjustified:

> *I am at a party. The party may be taking place on a boat. There are lots of people all around. To the left is a bar where I notice my grandfather (who is deceased) nonchalantly holding a cocktail in his hand. Then my step-grandmother appears. She comes over to me smiling, happy to see me. I say, "You look wonderful." And then I ask her how she is. She says everything is just fine.*

When asked about what preceded this dream, the dreamer related that she had been concerned over a boat cruise that her son would be taking the following night. As the cruise was sponsored by the International Cigar Society, the dreamer had envisioned that the boat would be filled with smoke. This thought gave way to a more troubling one: The turgid smoke would most probably make her son (a non-smoker) leave the smoke-filled interior for a stroll on the deck, where he could enjoy the fresh air. There might be crowds of people on deck and by some misfortune her son might inadvertently be pushed overboard. After relaying these thoughts, the dreamer freely admitted that her worry seemed unnecessary, yet she still felt ill at ease—until she had the above dream, which had the effect of calming her jittery nerves.

The dreamer's grandfather was always called by his

initials, I. G., and that the step-grandmother's name was Connie. For, during interpretation of the dream, as the dreamer put the initials of the two names together, she was amazed to come up with C. I. G., an immediately perceived reference to cigar. Then the dreamer reflected that the party in the dream may have been on a boat. Lastly, the dreamer was able to recount that the deceased couple were entirely at ease and that her step-grandmother said that everything was just fine. This was ample reassurance that all would be okay.

Indeed, the following night the son went on the cruise as planned and, as predicted, remained on deck for most of the cruise; he had a charming, if non-eventful, evening. Thus, from a psychoanalytic perspective, this instructive visitation dream may be interpreted as the dreamer's way of calming her anxiety. The dream serves to exemplify how the unconscious mind deals with everyday stressors. In other words, either the dream is a coping response on the part of the dreamer or the dream is a measure of the deceased's wish to positively effect the coping means of the living via advance notice.

The following instructional visitation dream was dreamt by **Esther Raab**, a holocaust survivor, at a time when she was in dire need of the kind of confidence that is only induced by love, as this was the night before she was planning to escape from Sobibor, along with the rest of her concentration camp. Her dream is as follows:

My mother came to me and said, "I know you are going to escape tomorrow and you will be all right!" She took my hand and showed me how I would go over the fence. And she said that I could stay in a small barn with hay in it, and that I would be safe. (I escaped safely but never found the barn. I went back years later to try to see if there was one there, but I could not find out any information.) (As told to Eric Sevareid, heard on the History Channel)

In these uncommon, most unnatural, and ungodly circumstances and on the eve of such a dangerous attempt at escape, Esther Raab must have been angst-ridden beyond belief, fearful of the outcome, of the ramifications from such courageous defiance, and in desperate need of assurance. Yet, pragmatically speaking, not escaping must have been perceived as a fate worse than death.

In that the worst possible outcome would be to die, the dream attempts to minimize the effects of death by presenting to the dreamer her deceased mother, which, in itself, may be viewed as a defiance of mortality. Similarly, the word "escape" may be interpreted as symbolizing two different things: an escape through death wherein the dreamer, reconnected with her deceased mother, will be all right, or an actual successful escape from her victimizers.

When the dreamer's deceased mother takes her hand, Esther not only connects with the loving protective ministrations of her mother but also reveals, in recidivistic manner, the desire to be led. The small barn with hay symbolizes the womb and reflects upon the dreamer's desire to find a safe place to hide in. Yet we are also reminded of the nativity scene: the manger wherein the baby Jesus is born. There is safety in Christian imagery, as it represents a symbolic departure from Judaism and from being dangerously Jewish during Nazi occupation. The barn is the symbol of life.

Esther's instructional visitation dream is viewed as a coping device, as it serves as a rehearsal and imbues her with courage and assurance. The instruction or guidance within the dream, which later establishes itself as predictive, is what prepared a less-stressful Esther to accomplish her death-defying attempt at escape, as she was confident that she would survive.

The fence (which must be overcome, and which, in reality, Esther climbs over) symbolizes the demarcation line between freedom and captivity, heaven and hell.

A most interesting instructional visitation dream was dreamt by a woman in England, who had remembered that her husband was in possession of a tape he had filmed of historical footage of the survivors of the *Titanic* being interviewed as they landed in New York harbor. He had filmed this never-before-seen tape when he had worked for a movie company many years ago. In that the blockbuster movie *Titanic* was playing in theaters everywhere, the woman rightly thought that the tape would be well received by an interested public.

But her husband was deceased, and she had no way of knowing what he had done with the tape. One night, after many days of serious looking, before the woman went to sleep she spoke aloud to her deceased husband and asked him the following question, "Tell me where the tape is. I have been looking everywhere, but I cannot find it." That night, as if in answer to her request, she dreamt the following instructional visitation dream:

A voice (my husband's voice) said to me, "It's in the shed under the bench." When I woke up, I found the tape exactly where the voice in the dream had told me it would be. (Heard on Access *Hollywood)*

A psychological interpretation would presume that the "shed" was symbolic of the unconscious memory-storage area where the woman would have to go to retrieve a piece of information she had stored years ago. As Ebbinghaus has written, because memories get covered over and buried under other memories, she would have to go digging under the bench to recall and retrieve what had been placed there years earlier. In other words, the information that the woman presently requests had been processed some time ago and was conscious to her in her frame of awareness, which is why it should be still accessible in her unconscious.

From a paranormal perspective, the husband seems to have made an instructional visitation, whereby he gained entrance into his wife's unconscious with the express purpose of doling out the necessary information.

DREAMS THAT PREDICT DEATH
OR PHYSICAL HARM

The following visitation dream is one that may be termed an indirect visitation, in which the dreamer views from afar his deceased father stepping out from the grave.

In 1849, several months after the tragic event of his father's funeral, five-and-a-half-year-old **Friedrich Nietzsche** had the following dream:

> *I heard organ tones as at a funeral. As I saw what the cause seemed to be, a grave opened up suddenly and my father climbed out of it in his burial clothes. He hurried into the church and came shortly out again with a child under his arm. The grave opened, he climbed in and the cover (sank) back onto the opening. At the same time the organ tones fell silent and I (awoke). (From Carl Pletsch's* Young Nietzsche)

In this frightening nightmare, which has elements of a negative-consolation love visitation dream, the wish is clear—Nietzsche wants to join his father in death. The father is viewed as omnipotent in that he is seen to willfully come and go from his own grave. This is meant to console and reassure the dreamer that death can be opened up or penetrated, that it is not a fixed state of existence but rather a habitude of choice. The grave opening symbolizes that the entrance to the world of the deceased can be broken into.

The father hurrying out from the church with a child under his arm, as though he has stolen it, symbolizes the loss of Nietzsche's childhood; Nietzsche himself is the child. Indeed, the father is metaphorically viewed as robbing Nietzsche of his childhood joys.

Yet, on the day following Friedrich's visitation dream, his younger brother Joseph actually died and was buried in the same coffin with his father, placed in his father's arms! What are we to think as we now reexamine young Nietzsche's prophetic dream? We can conclude that the dream was prophetic without altering the idea that Nietzsche's secret wish was to remain with and be protected by his father, for within the dream the child that is carried out by the father is literally carried off under his father's wing.

Yet Nietzsche's negative-consolation visitation dream may also be viewed as a fulfilled wish of Nietzsche's to remove his only male competitor from the Nietzsche household, for his younger brother Joseph's death makes Nietzsche the only male in the household. What is more probable, however, is that Nietzsche suffered from negative feelings of abandonment and lovelessness that make him dream of his brother (and not himself) being whisked off by his imposing father as the object of his father's affection and devotion.

At the end of Nietzsche's dream the organ tones fall silent, in sad symbolization that the music has stopped in young Nietzsche's life. When he says, "I awoke," it seems a telling realization, as if to say that he has awakened to the miseries of life, the sudden departures that leave one with feelings of loneliness and longing. Early on in the dream, when Nietzsche analytically says, "I saw what the cause seemed to be," he seems to be speaking about his own suffering and the negativity surrounding love, human weakness, and dependency— the hardship of mourning attached to the love of the departed. A philosophical aside: When Nietzsche loses his father, it is as though he loses God as well. His personal loss may have translated into his philosophical view that God is dead.

The following prophetic visitation dream was dreamt by **Heather Moore**, several years after the death of her grandmother, whom Heather never fully mourned at the time of the funeral because she was too self-involved with her life:

> *My grandmother was sitting in the back of a long, shiny, old-fashioned black Chevrolet that looked like a limousine. She had stopped in front of my home in New York to go to a movie with me. Somebody was driving, but I did not see the driver's face. She was seated in the back seat, and dressed all in black with black furs and diamond earrings. She was radiant and beautiful. I got in the car and we drove off. And then she said, "We forgot to get Aunt Jeanette." (Aunt Jeanette was alive at the time of the dream but died unexpectedly six months later.)*

The frightening image of a hearse is methodically transformed into an old-fashioned and necessarily long black Chevrolet—a shiny pleasure vehicle that drives the pair off to a movie. The movie, like the deceased grandmother, is symbolic of life based on the illusion of appearances.

The deceased grandmother is suitably dressed all in black, but with the prosperous accompaniment of furs and diamonds, as she still prospers (continues on) in the nether world. The color of mourning is vivified. The car gives the promise of movement to an otherwise deceased and immovable being, who appears radiant. Similarly, the movie reflects the movement of *reel* time, either a continuity of past, present, and future footage or a representation of the fictive, inauthentic realm of the non-real.

As a hearse is always driven by a driver and not a family member, the image of the chauffeur has been preserved, but not without remaining hidden from the dreamer's view, as Heather does not see the driver. In that somebody else was driving, the dreamer is driven most likely in an attempt to reunite with her grandmother, who she had not properly mourned in the past.

When the grandmother says, "We forgot to get Aunt Jeanette," the word "get" remains ambiguously ominous in the dream, in that Aunt Jeanette is still among the living. Here, the forgetfulness may reflect the dreamer chastising herself over having originally forgotten to mourn her grandmother and may signify that the living Aunt Jeanette is suffering the same fate of being neglected. Yet, in that the word "get" may be substituted with the word "take," as in take to the movies, we may interpret this word as a reference to the future death of Jeanette.

The prophetic element of the dream lies in the premature demise of Aunt Jeanette, who dies unexpectedly within six months of the dream. The consolation element of the dream is that the dreamer has not been forgotten by her grandmother, whereas Aunt Jeanette has.

PART VI

The
Prophetic
Gospel
According
to . . .

19

Jeane Dixon

rom the 1960s onward, Jeane Dixon has been known and on record for having been the psychic of choice for presidents. Her reputation for prognostication firmly established, she has had the opportunity to advise numerous politicians who were dependent upon her prophesies, and she has been successful in predicting some of their demises. Impossible as it seems, Dixon knew that President Lyndon Johnson would not be running for reelection before he did.

Most probably, living in Washington, D.C., is what allowed Jeane to become immersed in the energetic milieu of this center of political activity. Yet she claims that her gift of prophesy is not based solely on her receptivity to others' thoughts; it is also engendered by her strong religious faith and by her ability to read or interpret religious meanings in the thoughts of others. She modestly views herself as a vehicle that God sometimes speaks through during her daily meditations in the form of revelations. Over the years, Dixon has uncannily predicted that President John F. Kennedy would be assassinated while in office, that Senator Robert F.

Kennedy would never live to be elected President, and that an assassin's bullet would cut short the dream of Reverend Martin Luther King. Years ago, in the 1940s, Dixon was credited with having predicted China's movement toward Communism and the assassination of India's spiritual leader, Gandhi.

In an uncanny sense, it appears that Jeane has already seen the future (as in "been there, done that")—a future she is able to recount as if it is the past. In some mysterious way, Dixon seems able to experience events as though she has already lived through them, even though they have not yet occurred in the present.

Yet the gift of prophesy is a daunting talent. Dixon has spoken of the humbleness she feels as a result of her vast powers—and they are far-reaching. Jeane Dixon is in awe of her own vision or ability to hook into and ascertain the harmony of past, present, and future. In this respect, it is as if time is no longer visualized along linear lines but is rather circularized, in Einstein's sense of a continuous movement that spatially redoubles on itself. In other words, if one was to continue along a circular path, one would eventually arrive at a point behind where one originally started out from.

In Jeane Dixon's psychic landscape, there are no borders between the shore of wakefulness and the ocean of sleeping, but rather an overlapping of the two physical states. The ocean is the symbolic unconscious, and the earth is consciousness. Similarly, whether Jeane's forecast—her early edition of the future—arrives while she is sleeping or during wakefulness is inconsequential, in that all psychic activity traverses over energies that do not exist in time or space. We might say that predicting what lies ahead may be envisioned as entering a stream in the future and catching a big fish that is not yet born in the present, or viewed as entering a current spiritual stream where, without today or tomorrow, a big fish is snapped up in the eternal present. The revelations, visions, telepathy (thought transference), meditation, and dreams are all cut from the same spiritual fabric and are all texturally connected by God, for God is perceived as the essence, the Oneness, the knowledge within everything spiritual and prophetic. This is to say that although revelations and dreams appear in different realms of consciousness, they persist in being similar in that they are both part of the Oneness of God.

Dixon has stated that she travels between both realms (consciousness and unconsciousness) on a regular basis. Many of her dreams are filled purely with psychoanalytic content, while others are strictly revelatory. Both forms of dreams, however, should be interpreted from a psychoanalytic and paranormal perspective, for as we shall see later on in the text, there is some overlap between the two.

One of Jeane Dixon's most famous prophetic dreams foretold the assassination of Robert Kennedy. A paraphrased version of the dream is as follows:

I saw the biblical patriarch Job appear out of the distant past and walk up to a lonely Joseph Kennedy, embracing him with a tender, understanding touch. I turned toward Job and looked into his face. It was furrowed by sorrow and compassion. Streaks of dried-up tears showed on his sun-scorched face. I looked at Joe and saw that his face was distorted by anguish and grief. Uncontrollable fear showed in his eyes when he turned his head and recognized the face of Job. "What do you want?" I could feel his mind plead. "Why do you embrace me? What do we have in common?" Fright dimmed the majestic glow of the aura while

> *Joseph seemed to wait for the answer. But Joseph*
> *Kennedy knew the answer, and (within the dream) so*
> *did I!*

On a conscious level, Dixon has mentioned that she had always known that tragedy would stalk the Kennedy family. She had seen it happen to John Kennedy and psychically knew that Robert would follow. According to Dixon there are three levels of spirituality within her dream: 1) biblical references, 2) the dream state itself, and 3) the prophesy that is located within the dream rather than within a waking psychic state. What is interesting about the prophetic dream is its exquisite attention to detail, in images such as "streaks of dried-up tears on his sun-scorched face" and a face "furrowed by sorrow and compassion," which underscores the almost artistic sensibility and sensitivity of the dreamer. What is also present is analogous thinking, in that Joseph Kennedy is compared with Job. There is great empathy, the ability to feel what another is feeling (which may be a prerequisite of the psychic mentality), as the dreamer notices Job's sorrow and compassion and Joe's anguish and grief. Also striking is the seemingly poetic sense of parallelism in the wording of the dream narrative: Job and Joe, sorrow and compassion, anguish and grief. There is a meticulous sense of space, as Job is seen to appear out of the distant past. There is a simultaneous foreground and background as the past (Job) meets with the future (Joseph) already in possession of the tragic news of his son's death.

What is remarkable is that the dreamer looks "into" rather than at Job's face, in an investigative way that goes beyond surface observation. It reveals a direct form of understanding and signifies that Dixon enters at a deeper level of perception. She makes a sentient recognition or prognosis in the phrase, "I could feel his mind plead." The repetitious use of the visual or portentous word "showed," as in "showed on his face" and "showed in his eyes," is revelatory in nature; one would normally use the word "were," as in "were on his face," to communicate the existence of the tears and the fear.

Typical of prophetic dreams is that Jeane's place within the dream itself is minimal. This is because she is not at the center of the prophesy but rather is the medium who conveys it, the vehicle of transmission. Jeane, as dreamer, acts as a third-person observer and narrator, albeit not an impassive one, as she asks the powers that be for clarification about the dream content. The emergence of the biblical Job, although in accordance with her religiosity, may be viewed as a measure of conscious association between the two men, whose lives were similarly beset by numerous troubles and tragedies. As stated earlier, dream states and spirituality are congruent within Jeane Dixon's world, as they both are seen to hook into the spiritual consciousness of God. Thus, it may be said that Dixon views prophetic dreams as hermeneutic tools of religion, to the extent that they participate in linking the dreamer with the Oneness of God.

It is interesting to note the literalness of this prophetic dream; the meeting of Job and Joe is straightforward and simply stated—nothing is disguised. The interpretation is founded on the context of the dream and the narrative story that evolves within the propitious meeting of the two men. The dialogue is one of silent questioning on the part of the dreamer, who already knows the answers. Perhaps it is the intuitive intelligence of the prophetic mind or unconscious that has the ability to clarify emotional states rather than embed them in obscure symbols. Indeed, prophetic dreams are almost scientific in their prognostications, in contrast with the muddied retrospective revisionism of psychoanalytic dreams that deceptively reinterpret past events in elusive and distorted brushstrokes.

On another level of interpretation, we notice with interest that all names within the dream start with the letter *J*. Indeed, Job embraces Joseph in what we may assume as being the feeling of a kindred spirit. Jeane is linked to both via her strong empathy. It could be argued that Jeane is also symbolized by Joe, and that it is *her* mind pleading to Job "What do you want [of me]" and "Why do you embrace me?" as references to her awesome and sometimes frightening gift of prophesy. The questions go unanswered, for in the end they must surely be considered as a matter of faith.

There are times, however, when a straightforward prophetic dream should be analyzed from a psychoanalytic perspective as well. This is because the symbolism, imagery, and wording in all dreams is frequently easy to misread and even overlook. When Mildred Pickert, sister-in-law of Jeane Dixon, phoned from California to inform Jeane that her brother, Ernie, was to undergo surgery the next day, her call served as the daytime residue that brought about the prophetic dream quoted below, whose analysis, as we shall see, serves as an exemplification of a misinterpretation or misreading of a dream:

I saw Ernie and Mildred walking together. She looked extremely beautiful in a lovely bright-red dress with a high neck, flowing long sleeves, and a skirt that touched the floor. What impressed me most, though, was a candle she was holding in front of her. It was a short, burned-down piece of candle that I knew had once been long—very long. The golden flame flickered as she moved and went out altogether as she stood in front of Ernie. . . .

From this prophetic dream one is apt to wonder why Dixon rightly concluded that her brother's surgery would go well and that he would be all right. The most probable explanation is that her brother's wife depicts a festive mood, as she appears in a bright-red dress, which is certainly not the color of mourning. In retrospect, however, it seems that the dream was more about Jeane's sister-in-law and the feelings Jeane had about her, which would explain why the true meaning of the dream may have been repressed or overlooked.

The fact that Jeane neglected to notice that Mildred's golden flame went out altogether is quite revealing, as a candle is an obvious symbol of light and life; the light that is ominously snuffed out represents the darkness that follows and signifies death. The candle that is held in front of the sister-in-law represents the future, which becomes dark. The physical manifestation, the body of the sister-in-law (literally at the end of her wick) is completely covered over by her high-necked dress with long sleeves and skirt that touches the floor, as if she is already buried. Most poignantly, the psychic vision within the dream scenario would prove to be true, as Mildred dies soon after Dixon's dream.

The fault is not within the dream but rather lies entirely in Jeane's misinterpretation of the dream, which may have been caused by a disguised wish fulfillment. Being necessarily close with her brother, Jeane may have harbored a secret jealousy of her sister-in-law that may have manifested itself in the wish of her death, which would, of course, give reason to ignore the obvious sign of Mildred's demise.

Once again, we find Jeane is a passive observer within her dream, a bystander on the sidelines who does not even appear as a minor character. This time, however, there are no biblical references contained within the dream. Curiously, the symbolism, although plainly depicted by the lit candle whose golden flame flickers out, is strangely lost on Jeane, as she does not predict her sister-in-law's imminent death. In another view, perhaps because Dixon's concern for her brother was of foremost importance, it precluded all else, leaving her eyes blocked from the obvious prognostication. Perhaps the prophet must be willing to see, and it is a matter of will.

On a psychoanalytic level, the dream may also reflect Jeane's personal concern that her own candle may be burning low, an apt reason for this significant symbolic part of the dream to remain unnoticed or unrepressed. Yet this personal level of interpretation becomes irrelevant when the dream content finds implementation in the real world. The importance of the sister-in-law's death renders other subconscious meanings irrelevant, as the psychic energy of the dream-as-forecast bolts back and forth between the real and the metaphorical worlds, proving once again that Jeane Dixon is this century's prophetic *doyenne nonpareil*.

Regarding the envisioning of political occurrences, no one is in Dixon's league. In the 1950s Dixon predicted a protracted war in Vietnam, the emergence of Japan as a major economic power, continued turmoil in the Middle East, and the increasing threat of Red China. Now, at the turn of the millennium, we cannot help but feel that Jeane Dixon was here ahead of us, in an unknown, timeless, spiritual sense, and was only relaying back to us what she had already seen long before.

Of all of Jeane Dixon's revelations, she is perhaps best known for her prediction of the death of President John F. Kennedy long before Kennedy was even elected. The following revelation came to Jeane in a vision, or what I call a wakeful dream:

It was one of those drizzly mornings when I entered St. Matthew's Cathedral in Washington, D.C., for my morning devotion. I felt a glow of anticipation, . . . a feeling of expectancy, as if something momentous was going to happen and I would be involved. . . . I remember standing in front of the statue of the Virgin Mary when suddenly the White House appeared before me in dazzling brightness. Coming out of a haze, the numerals 1-9-6-0 formed above the roof. An ominous dark cloud appeared, covering the numbers, and rippled slowly onto the White House. . . . Then I looked down and saw a young man, tall and blue-eyed, crowned with a shock of thick brown hair, quietly standing in front of the main door. I was still staring at him when a voice came out of nowhere, telling me softly that this young man, a Democrat, to be seated as President in 1960, would be assassinated while in office.

Dixon has explained how the vision "faded into the wall, . . . into the distance as softly as it had come," but that it stayed with her "until that fatal day in Dallas when it was fulfilled." Jean's vision was basically a wakeful prophetic dream with audition (see Chapter 9, Vision as Wakeful Dream). Once again, Jeane does not appear within the vision. She is merely the visionary, rather than a character in her own vision, relegated to playing out the perpetual role of observer. Unlike a dream in which the dreamer has the opportunity to be visualized within the dream, she is not a character within her own drama. In that the key information was derived from the auditory rather than the visual sense, the vision is considered a passive wakeful dream wherein Jeane is the receiver. Most importantly, the voice is neither located nor recognized, because it comes from nowhere. But, of course, "nowhere" is everywhere in Jeane Dixon's prophetic world. Hers is an entangled environment in constant communication through God's presence. Although scientific explanations have been put forth regarding ESP, Jeane's beliefs are founded in the Bible, in Numbers 12:6: "If there be a prophet among you, I the Lord will make Myself known unto him in a vision, and will speak unto him in a dream."

How are these prophetic visions and dreams possible, as they defy the rules of scientific logic? Yet, even if explained, the question still remains as to the usefulness of Jeane Dixon's powerful prophetic visions, in that the visions were not given to supersede what must have already been fated. Perhaps the answer lies in the educating of our impoverished or diminished spiritual senses. Perhaps the individual vision is the tool that will nourish our belief in an afterlife and encourage us to look beyond the physical into the realm of the metaphysical, which is beyond our comprehension. Perhaps the prophetic vision is an answer unto itself.

20

Edgar Cayce

There is a history in all men's lives,
Figuring the nature of the times deceased,
The which observed, a man may prophesy,
With a near aim, of the main chance of things
As yet not come to life, which in their seeds
And weak beginnings lie intreasured.

WILLIAM SHAKESPEARE

According to the renowned twentieth-century Christian mystic Edgar Cayce, "Any condition ever becoming a reality is first dreamed." A strong proponent of the prophetic value of dreams, Cayce viewed dreams as a natural human process that, when analyzed, decoded, and understood, would be of great benefit to the individual dreamer in dealing with personal issues. While his many clients came to rely on him for his astoundingly precise and predictive analyses, they were nonetheless encouraged to develop their own powers of perception. It is Cayce's contention that an expanded self-awareness enables an individual to accurately interpret or ferret out a prophetic element in his dreams.

There is much to be learned from examining the manner in which this master of prophesy interpreted the prophetic dreams of his clients. It is known that Cayce placed himself in a sleep-induced trance, unimpeded by the diversions of consciousness, during which time he gave readings. He would listen to the recited dreams of his clients and answer their dream-related questions.

As unbelievable as it seems, these trance states allowed Cayce to enter not only the conscious mind of the dreamer, but also access what he called a universal information bank, from which he drew upon and found complete individual biographical histories—past, present, and future. Reaching this universal bank is what lent an uncanny accuracy to his clairvoyant readings. Perhaps he was just plugging in to his clients thoughts telepathically.

AN ACCOUNT OF CAYCE'S TRANCE STATE

The following is a record of Cayce's self-imposed trance state, as recounted from the notes of the Association for Research and Enlightenment, founded by Cayce in 1931:

I see myself as a tiny dot out of my physical body, which lies inert before me. I find myself oppressed by darkness and there is a feeling of terrific loneliness. Suddenly I am conscious of a white beam of light. As this tiny dot, I move upward following the light, knowing I must follow it or be lost. As I move along this path of light I gradually become conscious of various levels upon which there is movement.

Cayce continues to describe his encounters within each realm or dimension until he arrives at what he terms a hall of records. There, in efficient and expedient manner, a man conveniently hands him a book with information pertaining to the individual whose dream he is reading. Examining Cayce's trance experience from the perspective of what I call an actualized dream (see the chapter on Actualized Dreams in my book *Dream Keys: Unlocking the Power of Your Unconscious Mind*), Cayce's conscious action signifies a wish:

The act of lying "inert" in a trance represents the desire to leave the present reality. Interpreting the visual narrative is of particular symbolic value. The phrase "I see myself" reflects the importance of the narcissistic urge, and an obliteration of ego follows, as if in recompense, as Cayce is reduced to a "tiny dot"—a period at the end of a sentence, signifying the end of communication. Yet at this precise point of nullification, Cayce finds himself, proving that in order to learn, the self must leave the self. The oppressive darkness is an expression of the uselessness of eyes and foretells that Cayce will see in another way—through his mind's eye. Thus, vision aside, he is conscious of a white light. The light is God the father, as it is personified with knowing the way out of the darkness. Cayce is the son with the conviction of ascending the path of righteousness. He, like Moses before him, is given a book of information. Thus, he is given divine knowledge and the ability to give a reading. He is a modern version of Joseph, the prophet.

THE AKASHIC RECORDS

Cayce's universal information bank is actually the Akashic Records or what is believed to be the biblical Book of Life. Cayce describes the Akashic Records as containing "every deed, word, feeling, thought, and intent that occurred at any time in the history of the world. Much more than simply a memory . . . [the] Records are interactive [as they] influence our everyday lives, relationships, feelings and belief systems . . . [even affecting] the potential realities we draw towards us." In essence, the Akashic Records or world's memory seem another version of the Jungian collective unconscious.

If we envision the Akashic Records as an infinite chronicle of every soul that ever existed since the beginning of time, even in microscopic font, we are looking at an immensely fat volume of books! Yet this is Cayce's personal library and a testimony to his divine inspiration.

Many allusions to the Book of Life are found both in the Old and New Testaments. For example, Moses offers to pay for the sins of the Israelites by having his name written out of God's book; the Bible records that on Judgment Day Daniel and John see the books opened. It is Cayce's belief that only those who strive for an ongoing communication with God will attain access to the mystical Akashic Records.

CAYCE'S READINGS OF PROPHETIC DREAMS

Utilizing the information provided to Cayce from the Akashic Records, his readings were able to provide each of his subjects with a window of opportunity through which to view their personal circumstances from an entirely new perspective. Learning to recognize the prophetic element in their dreams contributed to their intuitive growth. Interestingly, during the years preceding the stock market crash, numerous clients—particularly stockbrokers, businessmen, and those in financial positions—reportedly had similar anxiety dreams about their various stock investments and about the general health of the market. This suggests that something was in the air, that there exists some commonality of prophetic intuition. The following prophetic dream of a financier, taken from more than 14,000 documented records of readings given by Cayce in his lifetime, was dreamt prior to the stock market crash of 1929. Harmon H. Bro, Ph.D., notes the dream in his *Edgar Cayce on Dreams*:

> A man fell asleep after reading from the Book of Ezekiel and "seeking aid from the divine." He subse-

quently dreamed of being held responsible for a murder he did not commit, and recalled the use of hypodermic injections in the dream.

For Cayce to interpret this dream as signifying the coming destruction of the stock market and to view the financiers as the ones using the hypodermic needle, trying in vain to inject new life into the market, would be astounding if the dreamer were not himself involved with money and stocks; the dream seems of a personal nature in that is it laden with guilt. The reading of Ezekiel reveals the dreamer's precognitive uncertainty and thus his wish to envision the future. The reference to hypodermic needles signifies the wish to get under the skin, to penetrate what is going on underneath the surface. Cayce assured the dreamer that through his solicitation of God he would overcome any financial losses in the future.

21

The Ancient Greeks:
Plato, Socrates, Homer,
Aristotle, and Hippocrates

The unexamined life is not worth living.

SOCRATES

A ccording to many ancient Greeks, man did not dream; instead, he witnessed divine visitations from the gods, who came bearing messages of warning or instruction. In other words, dreams were not differentiated from visions; the Greeks did not personalize dreams as coming from the individual psyche. Dreams were viewed as manufactured from outside rather than from within the mind, external phenomena that either predicted an outcome or suggested a course of action that would initiate the prediction event. In this respect dreams were always prophetic.

PLATO: REASON INVITES DIVINE INSPIRATION

Plato's position on dreams varied from this passive, noninteractive theory in that he empowered the dreamer as a visitor who could travel out of the body at night in search of meaningful messages and information from the gods. In *Dreamwork for the Soul*, Rosemary Ellen Guiley notes that this particular concept originally developed from the Eastern shaman religion and was later adapted by the Greek religious movement called Orphism. The Platonic dream ideal held that as the dreamer slept he entered "a between state," a place in which the human soul had access to divine messages. For Plato, the dream permitted man another way in which to interpret the world, in addition to rational thought and experience. By using dreams as an additional tool for exploring the intricacies of human consciousness, man could better grasp his instinctual nature as personified by the gods.

In *The Republic*, Plato refers to "those appetites which bestir themselves in sleep," in which the bestial virtue or "wild beast nature" of the soul (the pre-Freudian id) overtakes the soul's "rational" or tame nature (the pre-Freudian ego) in gratification of its needs. With the beast let loose, the rational part of the soul would not be free to travel at night in order to communicate with the gods. For Plato, a life of harmony and balance was a moral imperative. As long as man's appetites did not transgress or overwhelm reason, the soul would remain free to roam, to experience divine insight during sleep.

SOCRATES: THE MUSE INSPIRES THE MUSIC

In Plato's *Dialogues*, Socrates signifies that his dreams are divinely inspired by a prophetic voice that directs his creative energies. He does not consider himself the lone recipient of this gift but rather affirms that the prophetic gift is inherent in any great poet. In other words, "they utter their beautiful melodies of verse in a state of inspiration."

Socrates' last hours are recounted in *The Phaedo*, in which, as a prisoner, he expounds upon the conflict between pleasure and pain. Socrates wondered why Aesop had never personified either of these feelings in one of his fables. It was inquired of Socrates, who had never written a line of verse during his lifetime, why he had suddenly chosen to put Aesop's fables to musical verse. In response, Socrates recounts one of his recurring prophetic dreams:

> *Tell him, Cebes, what is the truth—that I had no idea of rivaling him or his poems; to do so, as I knew, would be no easy task. But I wanted to see whether I could purge away a scruple which I felt about the meaning of certain dreams. In the course of my life I have often had intimations in dreams that I should compose music. The same dream came to me sometimes in one form, and sometimes in another, but always saying the same or nearly the same words: "Cultivate and make music." And hitherto I had imagined that this was only intended to exhort and encourage me in the study of philosophy, which has been the pursuit of my life, and is the noblest and best music. . . . And first I made a hymn in honor of the God of the festival, and then considering that a poet, if he is really to be a poet, should not only put together words but should invent stories, and that I have no invention, I took some fables of Aesop, which I already had at hand and which I knew—they were the first I came upon and turned them into verse. . . .*

The dream always intimated the same thing: "Cultivate and make music." The word "cultivate" symbolizes the wish to humanize or bring life to that which is unborn or latent, and the word "muse" signifies the bearer of inspiration. As music was in itself considered divine, the dream may have been saying cultivate your divinity; the voice may have been Socrates' own.

To an extent, Socrates listened to his daemon—the

guiding spirit within his dream that appeared to him and gave the command—in that he expanded his creative self-expression through philosophy. He interpreted the word "music" to be a metaphor for his life work, philosophy. Yet, as recurrent dreams were given more import, with each successive visitation dream Socrates began to doubt his original interpretation. He questioned whether the gods would deliver such a powerful message if it were not meant to be carried out. This is why Socrates finally gives in to his creative musical urge and indulges his muse. He fulfills the prophesy by setting Aesop's fables to verse. In that Socrates never wrote anything down, one can see how strong was his need to heed what he thought was a divine decree.

HOMER: THROUGH THE GATES OF HORN AND IVORY

An explication of Homer's dream philosophy is found in his epic poems, particularly in his *Odyssey*. He believed in two forms of dreams that were passed down from either gods or demons. Regarding the truth and falsity of the dreams, those from gods were deemed veridical prophesies, as they passed through the gates of horn; those from demons were maliciously deceitful, having passed through the gates of ivory.

Ralph Hexter's commentary on *The Odyssey* reveals the extent of etymological play involved in the moral designation of the horns. The Greek word for "horn" is *keraessi*, which sounds like the verb *krainousi*, meaning "to fulfill" or "to come to pass," while the word "ivory" (*elephas*) is like the verb "to deceive" (*elephairontai*). There is also a visual distinction: The horn, in its translucency, allows one to see through into the future, whereas the opaqueness of the ivory does not permit an interpretation and is thus non-prophetic. Therefore, it was crucial that the dreamer be able to determine from which horn the dream emerged.

Homer understood the prophetic importance of dreams in understanding the personality (as evidenced in Penelope's dream within *The Odyssey*), as there was predictive information to be gained from an interpretation. Penelope's allegorical dream is as follows:

> *I have twenty geese about the place who pick up corn out of the water, and I amuse myself with watching them. But from the mountain came a great hook-beaked eagle and broke the necks of all and killed my geese. In heaps they lay, scattered about the buildings, while he was borne aloft into the sacred sky. So I began to weep and wail, still in my dream, and fair-haired Achaean damsels gathered round and found me sadly sobbing that the eagle killed my geese. Then down again he came, lit on a jutting rafter, and with a human voice he checked my tears and said: "Courage, O daughter of renowned Icariuis! This is no dream, but true reality, which shall come to pass. The geese are suitors: and I the eagle, am your husband to bring a ghastly doom on all the suitors." At these his words sweet slumber left me, and opening my eyes I saw the geese about the buildings devouring corn beside the trough just as they used to.*

Although a literary confabulation, Penelope's dream clearly demonstrates Homer's astute intuitive knowledge of the human psyche and the importance of prophetic dreams. The reason Penelope weeps at the death of her twenty geese is that she was secretly enjoying the attention of the male suitors. As the hook-beaked eagle is a sharp-sighted bird, it symbolically represents Penelope's husband, Odysseus, and reveals Penelope's fear that her erotic attachment to the suitors will not be overlooked but rather observed or found out. The phallic necks of the geese that are broken symbolize the conquering will of the Odyssean male phallus.

Although Penelope's symbolic dream is viewed as a direct and truthful message—a dream that should readily lend itself to correct interpretation—the far-sighted eagle analyzes her dream within the contextual narrative. A dream inclusive of its own interpretation signifies the importance of control to the dreamer—in this case, the blind Homer. The analysis within the dream also signifies an analytic mind at work. Thus, even as a literary device, Penelope's dream is prophetic of Homer's wish to help individuals not only understand the actions of the gods but their own actions as well.

ARISTOTLE'S PROPHETICS

Regarding the conceptual idea of the divine dream descending from the gods during sleep, Aristotle would have none of it, based on the fact that those receiving the divination were of the simplest and emptiest of minds. He theorized that visions received by frequent dreamers (particularly melancholic ones) were based on the frequency of their dreams. In other words, the prophetic vision came to pass as a singular or random lucky event or coincidence—if one throws enough dice, one's numbers will come in! Thus, Aristotle's belief in prophesy in dreams is thrown out the window in exchange for the belief in destiny or fate.

Without the involvement of gods or oracles, dreams were reduced to sense memories of perception made during wakefulness. Aristotle's pragmatic view is what enabled him to see the practicality in making one's dream happen. Aristotle viewed these "dreams sent by gods" as mere wish fulfillments. The foresight gained was concerned with things that were destined to occur based on the dreamer's active participation in the outcome. In other words, the dream is not divinely motivated but rather self-activated. The dream is the cause or initiator of what is created volitionally in a self-fulfilling prophesy.

Prophetic foresight in dreams is viewed as an indicator of the dreamer's keen recognition on a conscious level. What is needed is the faculty of observing resemblances, which enables the dreamer to make correct connections as though he were stringing pearls.

Aristotle did, however, believe that dreams accurately predicted somatic changes taking place within the body, in that during sleep the unconscious mind is more finely attuned to bodily changes than during wakefulness. Yet the divination or prophetic element stemmed from the physical organism, as opposed to any exterior god.

HIPPOCRATES: THE FATHER OF WESTERN MEDICINE

Noting a mind/body split, Hippocrates interpreted dreams only from a medical perspective. He viewed dreams as a vital diagnostic tool in ascertaining his patients' physical and mental well-being. In his *On Dreams*, the sleeping mind, unfettered by wakeful stimuli, is considered a master of perception of the subtle clues the body gives off to indicate its physical condition. The clues expressed through dream imagery and metaphoric symbolism reflect the condition of the body and mind and signal early warnings of illness. From this standpoint, the entire dream is visualized as a symptom. This philosophy, however, alludes to the prophetic functionality of the mind, independent and unaided by a divine power.

As the mind and the body are interdependent of each other, both parts must be understood if the healing process is to begin. Thus, Hippocrates valued the prophetic dream, as a by-product of the mind, as being able to access the general state of the psyche in diagnosing mental disturbances.

EDGAR CAYCE'S DEMONSTRATION OF HIPPOCRATES' BELIEFS IN THE PHYSICAL HEALING POWER OF DREAMS

Nearly two centuries later and on another continent, the mystic Edgar Cayce was able to prove Hippocrates' theory— that dreams understand the inner workings of the body and are prophetically diagnostic and curative instruments. It must be pointed out, however, that Cayce, in his self-induced sleep state, was brought into an uncommon super-unconscious— into a specific realm that he believed contained what he referred to as the Akashic Records, records similar to the Book of Life, which supposedly holds wisdom from the beginning of time.

As a young man of twenty-one, Cayce found himself stricken with a rare throat paralysis that, if left untreated, threatened the loss of his voice. His seemingly untreatable ailment baffled doctors. In the hopes of seeking to correct the situation, Cayce brought in a friend who provided the required hypnotic suggestion that put Cayce in the same kind of hypnotic-induced sleep that earlier on had allowed him to memorize his school lessons.

Under this hypnotically induced, trance-like sleep state,

Cayce learned of a physical disharmony within his body and successfully diagnosed his condition as a congestion of the larynx. His reading gave instructions that remedied his physical malaise. His unconscious knew what was consciously unknown. It recommended that he take specific medication and follow a course of therapy that would increase circulation to the larynx and restore his voice.

The Ancient Mystics: Buddha, Muhammad, and Confucius

The King of the Elephants, the Bodhisattva,
Casting off his jewels and costly garments,
Dressed himself in a poor hermit's robe,
the color of the earth, and from his body
there arose a light that dazzled the eyes of the Rishis.

THE GATHA

The miraculous events surrounding the birth of Buddha are foretold in the prophetic dream of his mother, Queen Maya Devi. In *The Marvelous Life of Buddha,* Maurice Percheron relates Maya's dream, which occurred at twilight, when the royal chambers were painted in a supernatural glow. Maya's amazing birth dream (transposed into the first person for means of clarity) is paraphrased below:

Four kings came into my bedchamber and carried me to a Himalayan peak, at the summit of which grew a tree. There, four queens dressed me in finery and led me to a golden palace where a white elephant with a flesh-colored head and with six ivory tusks carried a lotus blossom on the tip of his trunk. He offered the lotus to me and then gently sank one of his tusks into my side. He did not hurt me at all. (Maya awoke to the song of a bluebird and a feeling of "such joy as [she has] never known" and excitedly shared the dream with her husband, King Suddhodhana.)

After consulting with the wisest brahmans of the day, King Suddhodhana determined that Maya's dream was an omen that proclaimed the immaculate conception of his virgin bride. Queen or Princess Maya believed her dream was divinely sent as a message of annunciation that foretold the birth of their son, the Buddha—the Enlightened One.

Maya's dream is filled with sexual allusions: The tree, the six ivory tusks and the flesh-colored elephant's trunk are phallic symbols nonpareil that signify the virgin bride's mystification of the sexual union. The gentle and painless sinking of the tusk into Maya's side symbolizes her anxiety over coitus. Being entered through her side is viewed as a wish to keep her virginity intact. Yet within nine months everything happens in the way that Maya's dream foretells.

When Maya was about to give birth, she supposedly came upon a magnificent tree in the garden of her summer palace. As she reached for its branch, the tree (in personification) bent down to enclose her, and the infant Buddha was born from the place in her side where she had been pierced by the elephant. The tree signifies the tree of life from which life springs eternal. (Years later, another tree has symbolic significance in Buddha's life, for it is said that while sitting beneath the bodhi tree, Buddha found Enlightenment. Here, the bodhi tree symbolizes the tree of knowledge or infinite wisdom.) As the baby lay on a net of gold, four celestial devas (Indian divinities) dressed the Buddha in special garments and dipped him in the purified water of the spring. Four kings emerged from the heavens (dripping in allegory), showering the baby with flowers and streams of water.

It is conjectured that, with no assistance, the infant Buddha stood and walked as lotus blossoms sprang up from beneath his feet. Thus, it is no wonder that the overawed par-

ents named the child Siddhartha, meaning "perfect fulfillment." Prophetic dreams proved important to his spiritual
development as they gave young Siddhartha the determination to pursue his path as a bodhisattva, one who fore-
goes Enlightenment until all others are helped in attaining
salvation.

Siddhartha experienced his first prophetic dream telepathically. As Gopa (in some texts referred to as Princess Yasod-
hersa), his bride, lay sleeping, it is said that Siddhartha was
gifted with an ability to see Gopa's thoughts as though they
were his own. In that Gopa was at that moment sleeping and
enjoying the REM cycle of a dream, Siddhartha saw her
dream as one views a movie.

Percheron recounts what has been recorded in allegorical
legend: Siddhartha's telepathic account of Gopa's dream:

> She was watching a bull ram a barrier and push past
> some guards; the torn flag of Indra floating above the
> fortress turned into a fluttering banner threaded with
> silver. Then she was looking sadly at an empty pillow
> and a tunic that lay on her bed. Her couch turned over,
> her belt of pearls slipped off and turned into a serpent
> that kept biting her; her bracelets fell in pieces, and
> her jasmine crown was pulverized to dust. "The time
> has come," she sighed.

It must be reiterated that Siddhartha views himself as Gopa
and thus sees himself and his actions through her image
within the dream. Therefore, in Gopa's shared prophetic
dream, Siddhartha is the bull that pushes past the palace
guards to escape his penned-in royal existence. The torn flag
represents to what extent India has frayed, and symbolizes

the life of ruin and suffering endured by so many, a lifestyle that will be supplanted by spiritual salvation at the bodhisattva's hand.

The empty pillow signifies that Gopa's marriage bed will remain empty, and perhaps that a mind has been emptied of its dream or emptied in the way of meditation. The remaining material elements of their shared dream prefigure Siddhartha's Great Departure, for when he leaves home, he leaves his material goods behind on his way to conquering his attachment to worldly things. In symbolic fashion his mantle, girdle, collar of pearls, and bracelets are strewn on the ground. The hands are free of the entrapment of the bracelets; the circles are opened. The flowers of the jasmine crown are pulverized, returned to the dust of death in preparation of the rebirth of the soul.

When Gopa's dream ended, Siddhartha found himself bathed in radiant light, and he experienced the feeling that he and Gopa had become twin souls. As he stood by Gopa's bed, he telepathically communicated to her his thoughts. Their simultaneous dream was the presentiment he was waiting for; it prophesied his moment to leave and begin his religious quest. He interpreted a tear on his sleeping wife's cheek to mean that she had understood and accepted the significance of her dream.

THE GREAT DEPARTURE

Siddhartha's second prophetic dream was a wakeful vision that occurred at the onset of his Great Departure. In *Life of the Buddha*, Anil de Silva-Vigier notes that looking up into the heavens, Siddhartha saw many devas, who spoke to him. The following vision confirmed that his task was at hand:

The devas spoke to me. They said, "Holy Prince, the time has come. Now is the time to seek the Highest Law. Delay no longer amongst men. Abandon all, and lead a hermit's life."

It is said that the vision was preceded by celestial music and the showering of a thousand flowers from the sky. More than likely the celestial music was the sound of Siddhartha's inner harmony with the universe, the purring of the engine of existence; the thousand flowers was the unfolding bouquet of the stars that only seem suspended. With this divine message understood, Siddhartha made the supreme symbolic gesture of cutting off his hair and cutting himself off from mankind to seek religious enlightenment, as this would free him from life's suffering.

A BRIEF NOTE ON CONFUCIUS' VIEW OF PROPHETIC DREAMS

As the Duke of Chou, the mentor of Confucius, was known to visit his disciples within their dreams to guide them on a path of virtuousness, the absence of seeing the Duke within his dreams was thought to be prophetic of Confucius' imminent death. Michel Strickmann's "Dreamwork of Psycho-Sinologists: Doctors, Taoists, and Monks" recounts a Confucian statement made near the end of Confucius' life:

I am declining . . . It has been a long time since I have seen The Duke of Chou in my dreams.

THE PROPHET MUHAMMAD'S
NIGHT JOURNEY

Muhammad received his spiritual mission in a prophetic dream known as Israa (The Night Journey). The dream narrative, one of the most significant moments in Muhammad's life, outlines certain tenets of the Muslim faith that are later recorded in the Koran: God's laws of prayer, abstinence, and obedience. Betty Kelen's *Muhammad: The Messenger of God,* recounts a third-person rendering of Muhammad's dream, which below is paraphrased and transposed into the first person for purposes of clarity:

One night, as I lay asleep, I felt myself prodded by a foot. It was Gabriel's. I rose and followed the angel through the night streets to the entranceway of the enclosure of the Kaaba (the holy sanctuary in Mecca). There I saw standing, waiting, stamping its foot, a glorious milk-white steed—a magical animal, half mule and half donkey, with jeweled eyes, silken flanks, and wings neat against them. It shied as I approached. Gabriel said, "Shame on you, Buraq, to shy away from this honest man!" Buraq stood, sweating and trembling, as I mounted him. Then I, horse, and angel rose from the ground . . . and soared into the upper air, close to the lamps of the sky. . . . Every stride Buraq took carried us to the next horizon. Clinging for life, I was interested in the trek of caravans beneath, making their way to Mecca. We sped northward and eventually reached Jerusalem, the qibla [direction] to which I and my congregation turned as we prayed. There Buraq rested atop a hill beside a temple. I dismounted and entered. Around me I recognized a company of im-

*portant persons. Surely, all the prophets of the Book
were gathered there. The ancient preachers who had
gone before me and been persecuted and reviled for
their pains. And there stood our father Abraham, and
Moses, . . . and Jesus, a man of medium height, . . .
having a wet look, as if He had just come from a bath.
It was Abraham whose looks most arrested me, because . . . I never saw a man who looked more like myself! I was offered both wine and milk to drink.*

In other versions of the dream, Muhammad is offered
three beverages: "one of wine, one of milk, and one of honey."
The offering of three drinks is symbolically significant in
that it allows Muhammad to select the middle way between
religious and hedonistic extremes, a cornerstone of Islam. Of
the three fluids offered, milk is the only natural symbol; neither bitter and fermented like wine nor sweet like honey, it
represents moderation.

*I chose milk, and Gabriel said I was wise: "You have
been rightly guided to this natural drink, Muhammad,
and so will your people be. Wine will be forbidden you."
I left the temple and found Jacob's ladder erected before my feet, populated by angels. . . . I climbed it
through seven heavens to the very throne of God. . . .
On the way, the gloomy angel Malik, the one who keeps
Hell, lifted up the lid of that crimson pit so that I was
able to see the poisonous fumes leaping high and
greedy into the air. I saw men with lips like camels. . . .
In their hands were lumps of fiery stone which they
thrust into their mouths, and [which] would come out
of their posteriors. I was told that these were once
men who had sinfully devoured the wealth of orphans.*

*On the other hand, I had glimpses of . . . the worlds
beyond—. . . charming maidens . . . attended the couches
of the virtuous, unforgettable for their dark lips and luminous eyes.*

The inherent message of Muhammad's dream journey is
incorporated into the verse of the Koran: "Glory be to him
who made His servant go on a night from the Sacred Mosque
to the remote mosque of which We have blessed the
precincts, so that We may show to him some of Our signs:
surely He is the Hearing, the Seeing." The text serves as a remembrance of the experiences, some of which pictorially
vilified the evil doings of man and others that revealed the rewards of virtuous living.

The steed that stamps its foot represents the impatience
and demands of the dominating male ego. Muhammad bonds
with affirmative energy as he mounts the horse. In a self-
affirming gesture, Muhammad sees the magical animal shy
at his approach, as if in awe of Muhammad.

Of significance is Muhammad's journey to Jerusalem,
which indicated that God had designated it as the holy city
of Islam. By establishing Jerusalem as the qibla, Jerusalem
(for the time being) became the direction Muslims faced
when they prayed. (Muhammad later changed the direction
toward Mecca to distinguish Muslims from opposing religious sects.)

In the spirit of empathic camaraderie, Muhammad sur-
rounds himself with ancient preachers who came before him.
Although Jesus' stature is diminished as a man of medium
height, his modesty and humility is recognized. Presented as
looking wet, Jesus is viewed in a perpetual state of becoming, as water is the symbol of birth; water also symbolizes
the one who births or rescues and alludes to Jesus as savior.

Muhammad's facial resemblance to Abraham signifies his wish to identify himself with a great father figure. The encounter with the ancient preachers, most of whom have suffered or been persecuted for their beliefs, prefigures Muhammad's own persecution by his native Quraish tribe, who worship idols and do not accept Islam. Thus, the dream forewarns that Muhammad must suffer for his spiritual mission.

Climbing Jacob's ladder symbolizes the wish for ascension and also achievement, and lifting up the lid of Hell signifies the need to examine the darker instincts of men in admonishment. The glimpse of Hell warns of the fate of those who disobey God's laws; fiery stones excrete from men's posterior orifices in significant mimicry of their having rejected Allah's laws. This prophesies another passage in the Koran: ". . . whomsoever He causes to err . . . on the day of resurrection . . . their abode is hell; . . . We will add to their burning."

The dream envisions two paths: the hellish sights are balanced by the luminous and seductive rewards of virtuous heavenly life. However, in *Muhammad: A Biography of the Prophet,* Karen Armstrong recounts a different ending to the dream:

> [We] traversed vast stretches of heavens and approached the throne of God. God ordered me to pray daily. After some additional dialogue about the appropriate number of prayers, I resumed my flight back to earth.

In this version, the dream prophesies the number of daily prayers that are prescribed in the Koran.

23

Fellini and the
Prophesied Film

> Our dreams are our real life. My fantasies
> and obsessions are not only my reality,
> but the stuff of which my films are made.
>
> FEDERICO FELLINI

A follower of Jungian analysis, director Federico Fellini is a firm believer in archetypal dream symbolism and imagery. Throughout his life, they not only pervaded his dreams but foretold many scenes of his movies. Filed away in Fellini's extensive dream diaries were the makings of veritable screenplays. Thus, the dream was his muse, the predictive element of creative expression in Fellini's cinematic work. In his autobiographical account, *I Fellini,* the director confides that many of his best thoughts are unconsciously presented in images rather than words, in a visual panorama that is captured in his drawings during wakefulness. Remembered dream dialogue was placed over the dream character's head "in a balloon, like a comic strip."

Fellini was particularly intrigued by the Jungian concept of synchronicity (uncanny correspondences), as he notes that "coincidences [and] omens . . . [have] always been important in [his] own life."

In Jungian terms, synchronicity is a meaningful coincidence that reveals a symbolic interrelationship between the psyche and matter, the mind and an inanimate object or an event. Synchronicity is thought to have occurred when unrelated exterior and interior events become causally linked by the meaningfulness of their unexplainable yet symbolic connection. An event of synchronicity is to be found on the day that Frederick the Great died in 1786. Seemingly of its own accord, Frederick the Great's personal clock stopped at the exact moment of his death, as if in deference to its owner, for the clock had no more reason to keep track of time.

Meaningful coincidences are usually connected to archetypal symbols in the unconscious individual; for example, the clock that no longer ticks is a strong symbol for death. Interestingly, the Chinese theorize that science and philosophy are based on such meaningful coincidences. Indeed, there is ideational synchronicity within this chapter in that one of Fellini's dreams presented herein contains the symbol of a Chinese man.

Fellini's dreaming mind was filled with a plethora of fantastic imagery: the circus, the whore, whips, costumes, and breasts, among others. As we will see, these recurring images played an ongoing role in predicting scenes for his films. The following recurring dream of Fellini's, which he described as a "sex dream," was realized in his film *Otto e Mezzo*:

> *I'm a child in a tub being bathed by women. It's an old-fashioned wooden tub, like the one that was outdoors at my grandmother's farm, the kind we children used to mash grapes in for wine with our bare feet. . . . In my dream, as I get out of the tub, my naked, wet little body is wrapped in big towels by several women with huge breasts. Women in my dreams never wear brassieres, nor do I think brassieres that large ever existed. They wrap me in towels. They hold me against their breasts,*

*rolling me back and forth to dry me. The towel brushes
against my little thing, which flips merrily from side to
side. It's such a lovely feeling. I hope it never stops.
Sometimes the women fight over me, which I enjoy, too.*

In that Fellini's birth image is bathed in nostalgia, it resurfaces in his unconscious as the wish for rebirth and a return to protective immersion in the warm maternal waters of the womb. There is also the repeat performance of early childhood and its accompanying feelings of an all-embracing motherly love and attention. The young Fellini is wrapped in towels by mother substitutes in avoidance of an oedipal threat: several women with huge breasts. Thus, he is enveloped by flesh in another reference to intra-uterine life.

Yet there is sensuality as well. He gains sustenance from the large breasts as they invoke his erotic energies, his "little thing. . . [flipping] merrily from side to side." The dream signifies the dreamer's need to be dwarfed by an overwhelming largesse of female attention and nurturing.

Yet another inspirational predictive dream was incorporated into *Otto e Mezzo*. The dream follows:

*I was the chief of an airport. It was night, a night full of
stars. I was behind my desk in a big room there.
Through the windows I saw all the planes landing at
the airport. A great plane had landed, and as chief
of the airport, I was proceeding to passport control. All
the passengers from the plane were in front of me,
waiting with their passport. Suddenly I saw a strange
figure—an old Chinese man, looking antique, dressed
in rags, yet regal, and he had a terrible smell. He was
waiting there to come in. He stood in front of me but
spoke not a single word. He didn't even look at me. He*

*was totally absorbed in himself. I looked down at the
little plaque on my desk, which said my name and gave
me the title, showing I was chief. But I didn't know
what to do. I was afraid to let him in because he was so
different, and I didn't understand him. I was tremen-
dously afraid that if I let him in, he would disrupt my
conventional life. So I fell back on an excuse that was a
lie that exposed my own weakness. I lied as a child lies.
I couldn't bring myself to take the responsibility. I said,
"I don't have the power, you see. I'm not really in
charge here. I have to ask the others." I hung my head
in shame. I said, "Wait here, I'll be right back." I left to
make my decision, which I didn't make. I am still
making it, and all the while I wonder if he will be there
when I get back. But the real terror is I don't know if I
am more afraid he will be there or that he will no
longer be there. (Charlotte Chandler, I Fellini)*

The end of the dream includes an actual change of
scene, in which the director of the action is symbolized as a
ringmaster.

*The scene changes to a room flooded in great water
where I, in a ringmaster's top hat and tail coat, am
forcing a large rodent to swim in desperate circles,
urging it on with a whip. (John Baxter, Fellini)*

As an airport is a symbol of both arrivals and departures,
the ill-smelling Chinese man that arrives on the scene is reflected upon as being different, for he is the guide to the unknown, the Jungian shadow presence (the shadow is the
unknown man that consciousness must come to recognize),
an unacceptable part of Fellini that is neither understood nor

faced. There is the fear of incorporating into his life this shadow element, as it would mark a disruptive departure from his conventional existence.

The Chinese man does not speak through words but rather through a strong smell, signifying a fear that cannot be communicated in words but only sensed. Thus, an unknown quality is sensed and exposed—Fellini's "own weakness." Fellini's lack of decisiveness and action, however, is punishable via self-punishment: Fellini is portrayed as both ringmaster, in charge of the whip, and as a large rodent made to swim in "desperate [never-ending] circles." The ringmaster's tail coat is a symbolic reinforcement of the rodent's tail. The symbol of the circle is the Jungian archetypal mandala or the sphere around which everything spins, which represents the sense of contemplative self-awareness and the non-ego center of the personality.

The dream reflects upon the need for control in Fellini's conscious life, in that his unconscious, internal world sustains a sense of order by the regimentation of an airport chief and a circus ringmaster.

24

Freud on Telepathy

For more than twenty years Freud's supplementary Chapter C of his *Interpretation of Dreams* was supposedly lost or misplaced. The real reason for its long absence within the text was that it housed Freud's new acceptance of the genuineness of telepathy, a theoretical conception that brought protest from Ernst Jones, his editor. Jones felt this bold view would ultimately degrade psychoanalysis as a science.

The chapter, although dismissing prophetic dreams as nothing more than visualizations of the future that are linked to conscious calculations, "lucky shots," or falsifications of memory, clearly espouses Freud's belief in telepathic thought. Freud conceives of the possibility of telepathic messages reaching someone during sleep and coming to knowledge during a dream. He furthers this view by stating that telepathic messages received during wakefulness may be specifically dealt with during a dream of the following night.

As unspoken thought during consciousness is similar

to an unconscious dream, both thought and dream may be perceived (telepathically) by the sense perception of another individual, particularly if the thought is based on strong, emotionally charged content. The thought transference would begin at the precise moment when an idea emerges from unconsciousness.

The following is an example of a telepathic dream dreamt by **Hermina Rosenberg**, whose brother Louis was off fighting overseas in the Italian Alps during World War I, at a time when there was no communication allowed back to the United States:

I dreamt that my brother was in the Alps. He had crouched down to lean over a precipice, presumably to position himself for battle. He had a rifle in his hand. As he leaned over the edge a bullet knocked out his left eye, making him jump back.

On examination of this dream we are reminded that the locality of the dreamer's brother was known during consciousness, so it is not surprising that a worried sister would dream of her brother in the Alps, nor that he would be envisioned as crouching down—becoming less of a target—as her wish would be for her brother's protection. Similarly, as brother and sister were separated, the image of his leaning over a precipice symbolically reflects upon the large divide, the great gap between siblings. What is particularly indefinable is the clarity and exactitude in which this devastatingly conscious event was received by an unconscious dreaming sibling, for the event happened just as it was dreamt, and most likely at the precise moment of its inception.

At this time we may only hypothesize as to the existence

of a genetic link with the ability to transmit neuronal information such as intuited danger and acute pain at its shared point of impact. We would also need to theorize that traumatic events carry situational information across familial lines, or across strong, emotional bonds between loved ones. Scientific researchers have already noted the transference of stress across a long line of female worker ants that results in the last ant's unprovoked disturbance.

PART VII

Demystification

25

The Inside-out Theory of Prophesy

It has been theorized that within every man lies the seed of his own destruction. If this is true, it must necessarily hold that the seed, the determinant of the event, be known, if only on a subliminal level of perception, in order to establish a specific course of action that would bring forth such an outcome. This is the mechanism of a self-fulfilling prophesy. In other words, whatever happens in the future is of volitional intent; thus, it is made to happen from the inside out.

Several months ago, during the writing of this book, I asked myself before sleeping for a dream that would assist me in clarifying the mechanism of prophesy. To my surprise, upon waking the next morning I retained the memory of what I interpreted to be an initiation dream. It is recorded below:

I was in Lhasa being guided by an elderly Tibetan monk who bore a striking resemblance to my acupuncturist, Dr. Fill. Village people were walking around eating with chopsticks from hand-held rice bowls. I asked my guide what was the main food of his province. I said, "There is no meat, is there?" He motioned for me to follow him, saying, "I have something to show you." Through an open gate he showed me rows and rows of tall wheat stalks growing in the fields. He drew my attention to one particular stalk of wheat. He sliced the stalk lengthwise from top to bottom, revealing its inside, and I beheld a metal instrument, for within the stalk of wheat was its thresher, or that which cut it down. Within the dream I marveled at the insight: I took this to mean that within man lies the seed of his own destruction.

During my interpretation of the preceding dream I had the distinct impression that the dream was answering my question. It was inspirational in nature, as it filled me, as it were, with food for thought, bringing with it a new understanding of the prophesy mechanism. This was the meat of the dream that the guide was to show me. If we start with the premise that within man is the knowledge of his destiny then on a subliminal level man must know or have a sense of his final demise in order to follow a designated course of action.

Let us suppose that this inner sense or obscure recognition is a sound bite that emits from inside the mind and commingles with the air waves of the universe. Now let us assume that on some level President John F. Kennedy had the awareness of his future assassination via what I call the subliminal intuitive factor, and let us further assume that at the precise moment his sense reached consciousness it was released into the electromagnetic atmosphere.

No longer constrained, the sense-turned-thought is viewed as a liberated medium of intuition. Externally projected, it is caught within the psychic mind of Jeane Dixon (see Chapter

19), who then views it like a coming attraction of a movie. This happens in the temporal present and has nothing to do with the future, as commonly assumed.

What has occurred here is lateral telepathy. The sense of a thought has traveled along the plane of the present (see the figure). In other words, that which is sensed releases in the form of a thought. In the same way that unconscious content enters into the conscious mind through dreams, sense-thoughts may enter into another individual's consciousness. In other words, certain critical intuitive senses materialize between the material world and the world of the psyche.

It is theorized herein that everyone has a sending device—a subliminal intuitive factor—with the ability to exteriorize one's intuition, which is sensed rather than thought. On its journey outward, the intuited sense leaves the mind and is intercepted telepathically by a receiving device, common in psychic receivers such as Jeane Dixon.

SUBLIMINAL INTUITIVE FACTOR

SENDER: John Kennedy's S.I.F.   RECEIVER: Jeane Dixon, Psychic

The Present   •---------------------------•

Interestingly, although Aristotle did not believe in telepathic thought, he did theorize that sleepers could receive within their dreams the movements or thought waves emanating from other individual psyches.

26

Decoding Your Dream: Basic Steps

1. Always write down what you were doing the day before the dream (the day residue or antecedent).

2. Always establish the locale of the dream and the time frame.

3. Establish character delineation (who plays who); remember that you may be more than one character in your dream, regardless of gender or species.

4. Examine what is happening in your life.

5. Ask yourself if there is any question you want answered.

6. Establish your emotional state (glad, sad, guilty, frightened, jealous, angry, frustrated, etc.).

7. Circle all symbols (boat, sun, table, tree, etc.) and on a separate paper copy down the symbols and place equal signs next to them, then define what they mean to you. Think associations.

8. Examine the wording and underline any cliché.

9. Look for any phonetic associations (for example: blue/blew, chased/chaste).

10. Look at names of individuals who may represent others with the same name. Notice initials as well, including the initials of objects, particularly if the object, image, or symbol does not mean anything to you. For example: that "big box" in your dream may only be there to represent the initials B.B, which might be the initials of your ex-boyfriend or girlfriend.

11. Watch for distortions in which something is given major importance instead of minimalized; projections in which the subject of a proposition becomes transposed with the object—in other words, in which we make someone else feel about us what we feel about them (for example: "I love you" becomes "You love me"); reaction formation, in which the predicate of the proposition is transposed into its opposite (for example: "I love you" becomes "I hate you"); displacements, in which something becomes something else; reversals, in which order or logic is reversed; or word play, in which names have hidden meanings.

MY INTERPRETATION OF CAYCE'S GUIDE TO DEVELOPING PSYCHIC ABILITIES

Based on the belief that everyone has inherent psychic abilities, and thus a deeper purpose in life to learn how to use one's intuitive sense, Edgar Cayce hypothesized that everyone has prophetic dreams and that everyone would benefit from understanding how to interpret them. Yet, as there are steps beneath every great leap, one must begin at the beginning to achieve an inner faith. Here are some steps to climb during your ascent:

1. Begin by making a commitment to love yourself and others. No easy task, this. For only a selfless nature brings one closer to God. Your goal is a higher level of consciousness.

2. Drop your head and slowly roll it around. Listen to the release of the tension in your neck. Relax your muscles and let your hands fall at your side. Visualize yourself floating through what Cayce calls Universal Energy, or imagine yourself floating downstream on a large, unsinkable pillow. Feel yourself a part of God's light and love.

3. Light a candle and watch the flickering as it licks your skin, then *feel* the flickering!

4. Breathe slowly, thoughtfully, and deeply. Now eliminate the thought and become part of the process.

5. Eliminate all distractions. Contemplate and enjoy the silence. Focus your mind on one peaceful thought or image.

6. Begin to meditate. You may say a simple prayer or affirmation, such as "I am at peace." Such is the power of words that the right ones can deliver the sense or emotion you are looking for. It is best to empty your mind of all thoughts—to pull the plug on the computer so to speak—but this is difficult. Why are the easiest things so difficult to accomplish? *Because trying is involved.* Simply, do not try. Pretend you are a tree in the park among other trees, without any personality.

7. If your mind wanders during meditation, attend to your breath and repeat an affirmation. Focus on the meaning behind it.

8. Try to meditate for fifteen minutes at a time, but ten will do. Do not think of the time, however; just stop when you feel ready to stop. Then you may look at the clock and see how long you were meditating. Eventually you will develop a sense of how much time has gone by. You will not even need your clock. You will become more intuitive and attuned to existence.

9. Practice letting go—of anger, grudges, fear, and anxiety. When you let go you are able to receive.

10. Tend to your health. Preserve your well-being, your mental and physical body. Cayce writes that imbalances can distort "paranormal" occurrences or what I would call extra-intuitive senses.

11. Be willing to have God work through you and not *on* you. Cayce believes that during sleep we are in closer contact with God.

CAYCE'S GUIDE TO INTERPRETING YOUR PROPHETIC DREAMS

1. Bring to mind any impressions, questions, or unresolved issues before falling asleep.

2. Keep a dream journal near your bedside. Upon awakening, write down everything you remember about your dream.

3. Examine every relevant aspect of your present life: personal, domestic, financial, physical, and spiritual. Note any correlation to your dream.

4. Look for symbols in your dream. The more you learn about yourself, the easier it will be to interpret these symbols in a uniquely personal way. (This means you should make associations with your symbols and images.)

5. Notice any new perspective you get from your dream—any new way of looking at things, circumstances, or attitudes. Act on these insights in a positive manner. In other words, try to look at a situation differently, from odd angles, and if you should happen to envision a surrealistic scene, step into it in a creative way. Do not be afraid to get wet by the paint of your imagination.

6. Learn to trust your intuition. This will result in a

deeper understanding of your unconscious mind. After all, intuition is wired in at birth, and you should understand it by now. It has matured and is past the hand-holding, spoon-feeding stage. It is instinctual. Let it be.

7. Follow these steps in a continued aspiration for spiritual growth. Your reward is the achievement of new levels of insight. This results in a deeper, more prophetic understanding of your dreams.

Note: You must trust the veridical nature of your dream, as your unconscious is far greater than your conscious mind. After all, your unconscious has the stored knowledge of everything you have ever known, sensed, experienced, recognized, and perceived. Cayce believes that the unconscious holds the Akashic Records or has the ability to tap into them. Similar to the Jungian collective unconscious, the Records are believed to contain the whole of the world's wisdom from the beginning of creation and including past, present, and future. In a scientific evolutionary model, the Akashic Records would be viewed as "Ontology recapitulates philogeny," in which the human fetus goes through every phase of evolution during its development, acquiring knowledge along the way. In biblical terms, the Akashic Records are the Book of Life.

27

How to Interpret Dream Symbols

The following list of dream symbols may be used as a guide to help you interpret your own dream symbolizations. This list makes no claim, however, to exclusivity of meaning. Because dream symbols are complex entities, they are literally more than meets the eye and thus open to subjective interpretation. Each symbol, therefore, must be analyzed as it applies to each specific dream. The very meaning of a symbol may change or become modified by its relationship to the dream narrative as a whole, to the dream motif, and to its correspondence with the other symbols within the dream text.

Clearly, in regard to such commonly known inanimate objects as mirrors that reflect or windows that open and environmental features that are globally recognized and understood (oceans and trees), there is a certain dimension of universality through which the general public shares perceptive agreement and cognitive attitudinal response. However, even here we are faced with the possibility that many well-known objects are emotionally loaded symbols for specific individuals.

A passage in Jung's *Dreams* concerns a dreamer who dreamt of a table. Jung informs us that this seemingly unambiguous table was one that had particular significance for the dreamer, as this was the table at which the dreamer's father had sat when he chastised his son for being a wastrel and cut him off financially, which had the effect of forever making the table an unpleasant symbol of the son's worthlessness. This passage also reveals how life situations are remembered and recorded by the brain as if they are audio-visual scenes shot for a movie—scenes that incorporate the whole picture, the environment, the images, the moving figures, and the dialogue that determines the mood of the situation.

This is why when we reflect on our dreams we must remember that our dreams have been recalled from our past, a past laden with symbols that are temporally meaningful yet often inaccessible. We must define our dream symbols, make appropriate associations, and be satisfied with the fact that there can be no wrong dream interpretations, for each interpretation represents a certain level of personal understanding and thus a hidden part of our self that is now revealed.

APPENDIX A

DREAM SYMBOLS

Above: consciousness

Aisle: pathway; walking down the aisle: spiritual bonding, vows, commitment, dedication of purpose; *(phonetic— I'll; assertion)*

Alien: a deceased being; one who feels alienated

Animal: religious or spiritual being; instinctual nature

Arch, archway: rite of passage

Architectural structures: body parts

Arms: weaponry; physical protection; embracing love; *(phonetic—alms; gifts given in charitable spirit)*

At sea: not on solid ground; without understanding

Awakening: recognition, illumination

Baby: achievement; body of work; creation, creative process

Back seat: being driven, not in control

Background: past life

Backstage: the unconscious

Backyard: your own turf

Ball: sphere, world; self-concept, as point around which everything revolves

Barefoot: baring one's soul; getting in touch with the earth, instinctual nature

Basement: the unconscious

Bathroom: womb symbol; relief, cleansing; bathroom stall; begging for time

Beach: encampment; solitude, peace

Beasts: individuation; breaking away from norms; animal instincts

Behind: past

Below: the unconscious

Bench: permanence; inactivity, to keep from moving

Bikini-clad woman: the *anima*, female element in male unconscious; goddess as guide

Black dog: instinctual desires; symbol of foreboding death (emotional or physical)

Blanket: security, comfort, protection

Blind: lack of vision, foresight, faith

Blue: the unknown (into the blue); truth, spirituality; sadness; *(phonetic—blew; gone)*

Boat: foundation of life; conveyance; boat arrival: rite of passage

Book: of life; self-discovery, pages unread within the dreamer; gospel

Bracelet: that which encircles and restricts

Bridges: connections to another world, another level of understanding

Briefcase: a philosophy of ideas

Bright lights: fame; blindness; exposure

Broken window: self-destruction; emotional upheaval; inner turmoil

Bugs: babies

Building: the self; creative impulses; constructive outlook

Bunk: unification; steadfastness

Bushes: subterfuge, concealment; submerged sexual urges; sexual genitalia

Calling card: sense of identity

Camel: beast of burden; responsibility

Camp: staying entrenched in youthful exuberance and spirit

Candles: optimism; illumination

Car: drive; inside a specific world

Cartoon: omnipotence

Cashier, check-out people: being checked out, taken stock of; adding things up

Castle: the body; loftier, mature sense of self

Caverns: female genitalia

Ceiling: limiting factor

Chair: permanence; solidity

Chalk-lines: death; looking for answers

Chased: sense of being pursued; *(phonetic—chaste; morally and ethically pure, modest)*

Circle: concept of self; totality, wholeness; timelessness, continuance; mandala

Cities: symbolic of dreamer

Climbing (or climbing stairs): sexual activity; ascension in religious sense; achievement

Collapsing: sexual culmination

College course: the course of life; learning; introspection

Columns: body or body parts; phallic symbol; as architectural structure—standing tall; supportive; upholding ideals, order

Conductor: energizer, conduit; one who runs things

Corners: the four points of reference in the world; totality, wholeness

Costume: disguise, deception; roles we assume

Coverings: layers of memory

Crib: safety zone; protection

Crumpling: sexual culmination

Cutting hair: castration, losing power; sacrifice; physical or emotional detachment

Dancing: sexual activity

Darkness: ambivalence

Datebook: passage of time; agenda, schedule; self-identity

Deep water: trouble

Demons: primitive instincts; repressed sexual urges

Descending: quest for self-knowledge, self-discovery; the unconscious

Devils: tempters, protagonists, seducers; negativity, hopelessness; falling out of favor; negative *animus*, the male element in the female unconscious

Diagnosis: ongoing analysis in dream

Digging: self-discovery

Dinner: emotional nourishment or protection; satisfaction of needs

Dog: Dionysian animal spirit; instincts; making friends with yourself; foreboding one's death

Dolls: babies

Door: entrance to illumination, imagination; opening up or closing off; forbidden

Doorknob: phallic symbol

Drive (*as to drive a car*): ambition

Driving wheel: wheel of life; symbol of control, responsibility

Drowning: suffocation by system; being engulfed or over-whelmed; loss of identity

Drum roll: performance

Dust: layers of memory, veil

Edge: edginess; borderline

Elevator: that which elevates

Elephant trunk: phallus

Elephant tusk: phallus

Empire State Building: phallus

Empty hole: the unconscious

Envelope: deliverance; enveloped, consumed, sealed off

Excrement: death, decay, defilement; money

Excretion: the rejection or discarding of an idea or command

Explosions: sexual activity, ejaculation, orgasm, sexual climax

Extended objects: phallus; full-growth potential

Falling: surrender to an erotic temptation; loss of control

Fertile ground: womb

Film: distortion; veiled layer; projection of fantasy; raises identity issues

Fire: frenzied or ceaseless activity; intellect; sexual energy, desire, passion

Firearms: phallic symbols

Floating: on top of situation; above surface, superficial, without depth

Floor: levels; *(phonetic—flaw; defect)*

Fly wearing a sombrero: Spanish fly; being manipulated and controlled via drugs

Flying: freedom; renunciation; independence, detachment, objectivity; defiance of rules; exoneration; elevation and ascendancy; establishing individuality

Flying a plane: control; making all attainable

Food: emotional nourishment

Foreign city: womb

Foreground: present life

Forgetting: repression, frustration; fear of loss of efficiency or power of selection

Frog: evil spirit, historically linked to superstitions; something bewitched that was transformed for the worse

Front: the future

Front seat: womb

Frozen: stubbornness, resistance, rigidity, reluctance; inhibitions, fears

Garage: cemetery, graveyard, the underworld; the unconscious

Garden: cultivation of creative side, unrepressed nature, passion, spirit; origins

Glass: perception, clarity, transparency

Glass hall: perception of viewing or being viewed or watched over

God: the father, creator, eternal being

Going outside: independence, beyond confines

Grandmother's garden: womb symbol that skips a generation

Grass blades: weaponry

Green: novice, unripe, unseasoned, virginal; birth and fruition

Green pasture: affirmative view

Guns: phallic symbols

Hair: strength, power; if cut: castration, weakness

Handbag: self-identity

Harsh light: harsh realization

Hives: anger; physical eruption

Holding back breath: not accepting a situation

Hole: womb symbol; sexual genitalia; (*phonetic—whole; complete*)

Homes, houses: the body, the personality, being, self, state of mind (the more palatial the home, the grander sense of self); the mother, security, refuge; marriage

Hours: time element; *(phonetic—ours; belonging to union, partnership)*

Ice: the opposite of an erection: something that becomes hard in the cold; without emotion; linked to death, in that death makes things stiff; *(phonetic—eyes; being watched)*

Incline: struggle; maturational process

Interiors: the mind; introspection

Invisibility: unborn; protection; attached to forgetting or being forgotten

Island: isolation, independence, inaccessibility, autonomy; the individual self

Jesus: father, paternal figure; the good

Journey: departure, death

Jungle: the unconscious

Key: unlocking of higher truth, understanding; opening up

King: father

Knight: religious symbol as vassal of Christ; *(phonetic— night; darkness or solitude, as in contemplation)*

Ladder: ascension; attainment or accomplishment

Lake: reflection, giving surface view

Large audience: the eternal being; judgment; the desire to be heard

Leaning forward: letting go; trust

Leaves: something fallen; *(phonetic—leaves; goes away, exists)*

Left: the past

Light: consciousness, awareness; clarity of spiritual matter

Lighthouse: empowerment; scope; self-illumination

Lightning: bright idea; divine intervention

Little dog: helplessness, the underdog

Locusts: biblical: airplanes

Looking down: condescension

Losing a pocketbook: loss of identity; sense of violation

Losing a tooth: castration in men; being violated in women; a gap or void

Lynx: animal instincts; *(phonetic—links; connective symbol)*

Magazine: the self; storehouse of information

Makeup: covering reality; as in *make up*, or redemption, expression of sorrow; the sense of the imaginary, or pretending

Male hostile forces: castration fear, castrating father figure; negative *animus*

Mask: disguise, persona

Medicine: corrective measures; guidance; problem solvers

Mermaid: *anima* figure; female element in male unconscious; goddess guide

Milk: mother, maternal; natural

Mirror: self-reflection; looking for truth; imitation

Mist: blurred reality; *(phonetic—missed; longing, yearning, nostalgia)*

Moon: wholeness, luminous enlightenment, feminine presence, purity, ascendancy

Mother: one who births, rescues, creates, resurrects; mother's room, womb

Motorcycle: phallic symbol, sexual prowess; aggressive tendencies, drive

Mountains: obstacles, insurmountable problems; dominating presence; immortality

Mouse: prepubescent male child; phallus

Multi-storied structure: multi-faceted personality

Music: passions; being transported; sexual rhythmic activity

Nakedness: truth, purity, birth, innocence, naïveté; exposure; origins

Name: recognition

Nature: essence; giver and taker, hostile or docile forces, unpredictability

Nature trail: road of self-discovery

Ocean: psyche, soul; unconscious depths; mother; death

Ostrich: repression

Ovation: approval

Parked car: deceased individual

Party: celebration of life; complicity

Passenger terminal: womb

Pelican: scavenger, hunter

Pencils: phallus

Picture: the whole truth

Pimple: the wish to break out or leave; recognition of repressed anger

Playing: masturbation; motivation; free expression

Playing the game: living

Pocketbook: identity

Point: pinnacle; instruction or lesson

Policeman: the superego; dominating male presence

Pool: the body's internal fluids; amniotic fluid; above-ground pool: pregnancy

Precipice: on the brink of disaster

Pregnancy: filling a void, creative process, body of work; the death of a baby, the death of one's youth, fear of responsibility

Profile: not the whole picture

Puppy: baby

Queen: mother

Radio: the mind; transmitted thoughts

Railway station: departure or fear of death; appraisal of destination in life

Rain: birth, nourishment, purification, growth; tears, emotional outpouring

Red Breast: as bird, the female breast; the heart

Remedies: corrective measures

Repairs: emotional or physical imperfections

Restaurant: emotional nourishment; socialization

Ring: marital commitment, bond; wholeness and continuance, as in its relation to the circle

Road: quest for knowledge, freedom of expression; direction

Rooms: the body; the personality

Sand: restrictive side of reason; sterile, barren, abrasive

Scene: *(phonetic—seen; realization, recognition)*

Scenes: facades; memories

Scorpion: biblical—tanks; stinging, biting

Script: part one plays in life; meaning, ideology, philosophy

Sea: unconscious, immersion; *(phonetic—see; understand, recognize)*

See-through: truthfulness

Shoes: feminine genitalia; watching your step

Shrinking: sexual culmination

Silhouette: outline, only part of the picture

Skating: avoiding issues

Sky: without limit; open-mindedness; independence

Snake: temptation; transcendence over instinctual side, change, sloughing of skin

Sole: *(phonetic—soul; psyche)*

Space: void

Spear: phallus

Spheres: the world; seraphim

Spiderwebs: entrapment

Stadium: magic circle, mandala; wholeness, totality

Stage: set-up; platform for ideas; maturational phase of development; spiritual elevation

Stage manager: God; the father; parental figure

Stairwell: stasis, lack of extremism in either direction; moderation

Storm: stressful time

Striking: lashing out or not accepting

Summer: youth; blooming, burgeoning relationships

Sun: Christ; dawn, new beginning; the father; *(phonetic—son; male child)*

Surfaces: relating to sense of touch and feelings; superficial; to rise into view

Tail: *(phonetic—tale; story)*

Taxi: being transported; inside vehicle: a specific world

Telephones: communicators with the deceased

Tests: preparations; self-expectations

Text search: way out of conflict, looking for answers

Ticket: gaining admittance, approval, acceptance

Tiered seats: developmental stages of life

Tomb: womb substitute

Tower: body, aloofness, independence; spiritual or mental elevation

Train: phallus

Train station: departure

Tree: of life; creativity, fortitude, rootedness; phallus; union of male and female; marriage symbol

Tree branches: offshoots; alluding to evolution

Tunnel: womb

Twilight: neither here nor there; noncommittal; transition

Underneath: the unconscious

Valley: unconsciousness; mother, nurturing wholeness; depression, a low point in life

Video games: at the controls of life; maneuvered or maneuvering

Warm water: tears; rebirth

Water: birth; rescue, redemption, renewal, absolution; the unconscious

Waves: being swallowed up, washed over; waving, welcoming or dismissive

Weather: driving, changeable force; physical or emotional condition; *(phonetic—whether; indecisive)*

Wheel: the sun; divinity; wheel of life; *(phonetic—we'll; togetherness)*

White: purity; religious devotion; cleansing; truth

White House: the Presidency; leadership; self-enlightenment

Windows: the self, the soul; eyes of the soul; opportunities; as a breathing space: somatic of lungs

Wine: blood; life force; intoxication; (biblical—fermented)

Winter: death or dying; what is forgotten or covered over; old age; the deceased

Wires: wired-in, connected

Wise old man: guardian; God, spirit guide; *animus*

Witch: *anima,* negative feminine side of psyche; *(phonetic—which; involving choice)*

Wood: *(phonetic—would; involving the conditional)*

Note: Because certain dream symbols are emotionally loaded to certain individuals and particular to that specific person, dream symbols cannot be proven to be uni-

versally accepted truths. The dream symbols listed above are those that have already been defined in relation to their respective meanings within the specific dream narrations in which they appear, both in this book and in my other books, **Dream Keys: Unlocking the Power of Your Unconscious Mind** *and* **Dream Keys for Love: Unlocking the Secrets of Your Own Heart.**

APPENDIX B

DREAM JOURNAL TO RECORD YOUR DREAMS			
Date	*Dream Narrative*	*Emotional Reaction*	*Antecedent*

Date	Dream Narrative	Emotional Reaction	Antecedent

Date	Dream Narrative	Emotional Reaction	Antecedent

Date	Dream Narrative	Emotional Reaction	Antecedent

BIBLIOGRAPHY

Karen Armstrong, *Muhammad: A Biography of the Prophet* (San Francisco: Harper, 1992).

John Baxter, *Fellini* (New York: St. Martin's Press, 1993).

John Beevers, *St. Joan of Arc* (Garden City, New York: Hanover House, 1974).

Harmon H. Bro, Ph.D., *Edgar Cayce on Dreams* (New York: Warner Books, 1968).

Charlotte Chandler, *I, Fellini* (New York: Random House, 1995).

Ron Chernow, *Titan* (New York: Random House, 1998).

Anil de Silva-Vigier, *Life of the Buddha Retold from Ancient Sources* (London: Phaidon Press, 1955).

W. C. Dement, *The Functions of Sleep* (New York: Academic Press, 1979).

Jeane Dixon, *My Life and Prophecies: Her Own Story as Told to Rene Noorberger* (New York: William Morrow and Company, Inc., 1969).

Naomi Epel, *Writers Dreaming* (New York: Carol Southern Books, 1993).

F. R. Freemon, *Sleep Research: A Critical View* (Springfield, Ill.: Charles C. Thomas, 1972).

Sigmund Freud, *The Standard Edition,* Volume 21 (London: The Hogarth Press, 1975).

Eric Fromm, *The Forgotten Language* (New York: Harper, 1951).

Elizabeth Fuller, *Everyone Is Psychic, The Edgar Cayce Way to Unlock Your Own Hidden Psychic Ability for a Richer, More Rewarding Life* (New York: Crown, 1989).

Rosemary Ellen Guiley, *Dreamwork for the Soul: A Spiritual Guide to Interpretation* (New York: Berkley Books, 1989).

Brian Hill, *Such Stuff as Dreams* (London: Rupert Hart-Davis, 1967).

John Hogue, *Nostradamus and the Millennium* (New York: Doubleday, 1987).

The Holy Bible, New King James Version (Nashville: Thomas Nelson Publishers, 1987).

B. Jowett, *Plato. The Five Great Dialogues* (Roslyn, New York: Walter J. Black, Inc., 1942).

Betty Kelen, *Muhammad: The Messenger of God* (Nashville: Thomas Nelson Inc., 1975).

Morton T. Kelsey, *God, Dreams and Revelations: A Christian Interpretation of Dreams* (Minneapolis: Augsburg Fortress Publications, 1974)

Maurice Percheron, *Marvelous Life of the Buddha* (New York: St. Martin's Press, 1960).

Carl Pletsch, *Young Nietzsche* (New York: The Free Press, 1991).

Vita Sackville-West, *Saint Joan of Arc* (New York: Image Books–Doubleday, 1991).

William Shakespeare, *The Works of William Shakespeare* (Roslyn, New York: Walter J. Black, Inc. 1937).

Sven Stolpe, *The Maid of Orleans* (New York: Pantheon, 1956).

Robert Van de Castle, Ph.D., *Our Dreaming Mind* (New York: Ballantine Books, 1994).

Edward O. Wilson, *Consilience* (New York: Alfred A. Knopf, 1998).

ABOUT THE AUTHOR

LAUREN LAWRENCE is a psychoanalyst with a specialty in dream analysis. She is a regular on Joey Reynolds's nationally syndicated WOR AM radio show. Her column on celebrity dreams formerly appeared in the New York *Daily News* and her column on the dreams of famous political figures formerly appeared in *George*. She is the dreams expert of Dreamlife.com, an interactive Web community, and gives live chats over Dreamlife.com and Yahoo!

Lauren Lawrence is also the author of *Dream Keys*, the first book in the Dream Keys series, and *Dream Keys for Love*. She lives in New York City.

BANTAM NEW AGE BOOKS

A SEARCH FOR MEANING, GROWTH, AND CHANGE

Ask for these books at your local bookstore or use this page to order.

Please send me the books I have checked above. I am enclosing $_____ (add $2.50 to cover postage and handling). Send check or money order, no cash or C.O.D.'s, please.

Name _____

Address _____

City/State/Zip _____

Send order to: Bantam Books, Dept. NA 11, 2451 S. Wolf Rd., Des Plaines, IL 60018
Allow four to six weeks for delivery.

Prices and availability subject to change without notice.   NA 11 1/00